SCRIBBLES

God blessed me with the alphabet & an imagination.

I transformed them to words that paint a picture on paper to share with you.

Nonetheless, from God to me to you.

Xoxo tj

Scriptures noted Taken from KJV of the Bible. http://www.biblestudytools.com/. Copyright © 2013 Bible Study Tools. All rights reserved. Article Images Copyright © 2013 JupiterImages Corporation.

Photographs courtesy of T M Jones, Stephen Bruce http://scbcreative.com/, Patrick Jones spoone_ent@yahoo.com

Edited by T. M. Jones & Johnel Williams III (Trey)

Cover design by T. M. Jones

ISBN-13: 978-1491059692
ISBN-10: 1491059699

DEDICATION

My mom, Ernestine Gibson you're my biggest cheerleader. My dad, Cleveland Johnson who's never passed judgement on me. My children, Nique, Mari, Trey, & Bubba and all my extra children including Elijah & Diamond. My sisters, LaTonya, Vanessa, Marla, Mikki, & Angela. My nieces and nephews.

My pastor, William D Bishop & my Mt Ivory MBC family. The Union District churches who have invited me to share my poetry in fellowship & service.

My co-poets in the Lou (too many to name but my biggest motivators). Especially the venues who allowed me to grace their stage: Legacy Books & Café, Love Jones Theory, Hustle & Flow & all the other venues I've visited. My friends & co-workers & growing fans that have come out to support me.

THANKS FOR SHOWING ME SO MUCH LOVE

INTRODUCTION

I have several characters within this book. You will find Sweetness who speaks of erotica, Angel Wings who is very spiritual & motivational, Discombobulated who's is angry, and Simplexity who is a combination of simple & complex and tells a story or has no specific character or a combination of characters.

Instead of organizing this book by characters, I decided to organize in alphabetical order to take you through a variety of intriguing possible highs and lows and everything in between within all four of my characters.

TABLE OF CONTENTS

A Lil Frisky~~~~~~9

Abc's of Sex~~~~~~~~~~~~~~~~~~~~~~~~~~~~~~~~~~~~~~10

Art of a Circumcision~~~~~~~~~~~~~~~~~~~~~~~~~~~~~~11

Beatitudes~~~~~~~~~~~~~~~~~~~~~~~~~~~~~~~~~~~~~~12

Bipolar love~~~~~~~~~~~~~~~~~~~~~~~~~~~~~~~~~~~~~13

Box of Chocolates~~~~~~~~~~~~~~~~~~~~~~~~~~~~~~~~14

Boyfriend #1 & Boyfriend #2~~~~~~~~~~~~~~~~~~~~~~~~15

Butterfly~~~~~~~~~~~~~~~~~~~~~~~~~~~~~~~~~~~~~~~16

Can I Lay in Your Arms~~~~~~~~~~~~~~~~~~~~~~~~~~~~18

Crush~~~~~~20

Dem Bones~~~~~~~~~~~~~~~~~~~~~~~~~~~~~~~~~~~~~22

Desire~~~~~~24

Did You Get Fully Dressed Today~~~~~~~~~~~~~~~~~~~~~25

Don't do God no Favors~~~~~~~~~~~~~~~~~~~~~~~~~~~26

Don't Swallow~~~~~~~~~~~~~~~~~~~~~~~~~~~~~~~~~~28

Down On Me~~~~~~~~~~~~~~~~~~~~~~~~~~~~~~~~~~~30

Especially Different~~~~~~~~~~~~~~~~~~~~~~~~~~~~~~31

Fantasy World~~~~~~~~~~~~~~~~~~~~~~~~~~~~~~~~~~32

From a King To a Queen~~~~~~~~~~~~~~~~~~~~~~~~~~~34

Fuck You Very Much~~~~~~~~~~~~~~~~~~~~~~~~~~~~~~36

Fuque Love Son~~~~~~~~~~~~~~~~~~~~~~~~~~~~~~~~~39

Good Friends Have Your Back~~~~~~~~~~~~~~~~~~~~~~~40

Great Pleasure~~~~~~~~~~~~~~~~~~~~~~~~~~~~~~~~~42

Haiku & Other Short Poems~~~~~~~~~~~~~~~~~~~~~~~~43

He~~~~~~44

He Gives Me Fever~~~~~~~~~~~~~~~~~~~~~~~~~~~~~~~45

Healing Me~~~~~~~~~~~~~~~~~~~~~~~~~~~~~~~~~~~~46

Homeless Spirits of God~~~~~~~~~~~~~~~~~~~~~~~~~~~47

Hopeless Case~~~~~~~~~~~~~~~~~~~~~~~~~~~~~~~~~~48

I Am a Christian~~~~~~~~~~~~~~~~~~~~~~~~~~~~~~~~49

I Apologize to my King~~~~~~~~~~~~~~~~~~~~~~~~~~~~50

I Grieve~~~~~~~~~~~~~~~~~~~~~~~~~~~~~~~~~~~~~~52

I Just Wanna Praise Him~~~~~~~~~~~~~~~~~~~~~~~~~~~54

I Love my Brothas~~~~~~~~~~~~~~~~~~~~~~~~~~~~~~~56

If I Were the Wind~~~~~~~~~~~~~~~~~~~~~~~~~~~~~~~57

I'm Falling in Sprung~~~~~~~~~~~~~~~~~~~~~~~~~~~~~58

I'm in Love With a Man~~~~~~~~~~~~~~~~~~~~~~~~~~~60

I'm Obsessed With You~~~~~~~~~~~~~~~~~~~~~~~~~~~62

I'm Sick & Tired~~~~~~~~~~~~~~~~~~~~~~~~~~~~~~~~64

I'm Spoiled~~~~~~~~~~~~~~~~~~~~~~~~~~~~~~~~~~~65

I'm Tender-Headed~~~~~~~~~~~~~~~~~~~~~~~~~~~~~~67

In the Beginning God Created Sex~~~~~~~~~~~~~~~~~~~68

Just Rest~~~~~~~~~~~~~~~~~~~~~~~~~~~~~70
Last Night I Had a Dream~~~~~~~~~~~~~~~~~71
Lay Over~~~~~~~~~~~~~~~~~~~~~~~~~~~~~72
Let's Take a Trip to the Bathroom~~~~~~~~~~~73
Lord Help Me~~~~~~~~~~~~~~~~~~~~~~~~74
Love at First Site~~~~~~~~~~~~~~~~~~~~~~76
Love greater than eternity~~~~~~~~~~~~~~~~~78
Makin love with unspoken words~~~~~~~~~~~~79
Massa's Love~~~~~~~~~~~~~~~~~~~~~~~~80
Miss Happy Juice~~~~~~~~~~~~~~~~~~~~~~82
Mr A.M.~~~~~~~~~~~~~~~~~~~~~~~~~~~83
Mr Lewis Baker~~~~~~~~~~~~~~~~~~~~~~~84
My Prayer is to Heal the Land~~~~~~~~~~~~~86
New Beginnings~~~~~~~~~~~~~~~~~~~~~~88
Newly Found Love~~~~~~~~~~~~~~~~~~~~~89
No Weapon~~~~~~~~~~~~~~~~~~~~~~~~~90
Order my Steps~~~~~~~~~~~~~~~~~~~~~~92
Our Father~~~~~~~~~~~~~~~~~~~~~~~~~96
Pain Pleasure Bittersweet~~~~~~~~~~~~~~~~98
Press On~~~~~~~~~~~~~~~~~~~~~~~~~~102
Pretend I'm Her~~~~~~~~~~~~~~~~~~~~~104
Prince Princesses Kings Queens Rulers & Leaders~~~106
Purge~~~~~~~~~~~~~~~~~~~~~~~~~~~~110
Put Your Lips On Me~~~~~~~~~~~~~~~~~~~111
Queen of Hearts~~~~~~~~~~~~~~~~~~~~~112
Rebuild Me From This Brokenness~~~~~~~~~~114
Rebuke~~~~~~~~~~~~~~~~~~~~~~~~~~~117
Safe Feeling~~~~~~~~~~~~~~~~~~~~~~~~118
Secret Hug~~~~~~~~~~~~~~~~~~~~~~~~~119
Single Sexy Celibate~~~~~~~~~~~~~~~~~~~120
She Begged Me~~~~~~~~~~~~~~~~~~~~~~122
She Said & He Said~~~~~~~~~~~~~~~~~~~124
Smile~~~~~~~~~~~~~~~~~~~~~~~~~~~~125
Sniff ~~~~~~~~~~~~~~~~~~~~~~~~~~~~126
Spiritual Woman 3 Snaps Up~~~~~~~~~~~~~127
Spoon Me~~~~~~~~~~~~~~~~~~~~~~~~~128
Sticks & Stones~~~~~~~~~~~~~~~~~~~~~~129
Suck You Bone Dry~~~~~~~~~~~~~~~~~~~130
Taste Me~~~~~~~~~~~~~~~~~~~~~~~~~131
Thanks For Making My Day~~~~~~~~~~~~~~132
The Blood of Jesus~~~~~~~~~~~~~~~~~~~134
There is a Time~~~~~~~~~~~~~~~~~~~~~136
This Must be a Bad Dream~~~~~~~~~~~~~~138
Touch~~~~~~~~~~~~~~~~~~~~~~~~~~~~140

Touch of an Angel~~~~~~~~~~~~~~~~~~~~~~~141
Trifling Ass~~~~~~~~~~~~~~~~~~~~~~~~~~~142
Turbulence~~~~~~~~~~~~~~~~~~~~~~~~~~~144
Type of Love Too~~~~~~~~~~~~~~~~~~~~~~146
Ur Beautiful~~~~~~~~~~~~~~~~~~~~~~~~~148
We Danced~~~~~~~~~~~~~~~~~~~~~~~~~~149
Wet Daydreams~~~~~~~~~~~~~~~~~~~~~~~150
What Just Happened?~~~~~~~~~~~~~~~~~~~151
What Manner of Man is This?~~~~~~~~~~~~~~152
What's Wrong Witcha~~~~~~~~~~~~~~~~~~~155
When a Tree Falls~~~~~~~~~~~~~~~~~~~~~156
Who Knew?~~~~~~~~~~~~~~~~~~~~~~~~~~157
Why do we Sing~~~~~~~~~~~~~~~~~~~~~~158
Woo man.....~~~~~~~~~~~~~~~~~~~~~~~~~159

A LIL FRISKY

....if he could just lightly kiss the back of my neck
....if he could just rub my arm & make me feel like silk
....if he could just lick my breast like a melting ice cream cone
....if he could put his tongue in my navel
....if he could just kiss my ass and put a hickey there
....if he could just gently put my ankle around his neck
....if he could take his thumb & his index finger massage my cookie
....if he could only exist

so until then, I've got to wash my hair....smile

ABC's of Sex

A – apple bottom, aphrodisiac, anal
B – bubble bath, breast, bondage, blindfold
C – climax, cum, car, chair
D – doggy style
E – ejaculations, erection
F – fingering, Fredrick's of Hollywood
G – g-spot
H – hot
I – intimacy
J – juices
K – knees
L – lips, labia, lick
M – mirrors
N – nymphomaniac
O – oral, open, orifice
P – punany, poles, penis, paddle, plug
Q – quivering
R – romance, rim shot, roses,
S – sucking, spanking, shower
T – testicals, teeth, toes, twirp, tub
U – u-spot
V – video tape, Victoria secret
W – whip
X – x-rated
Y – y u gotta cum so fast
Z – zane

ART OF A CIRCUMCISION

When baby boys are born they are usually circumcised within a
week
Strapped down on the table: head, arms, waist, knees & feet
Generally no anesthesia is used
An instrument called plastibell or mojen clamp is used
Poor lil baby look like he's about to be abused
Put the instrument around the penis, pull up on the foreskin
Clamp it down & lock. Then a scalpel is used to cut & excised the
access skin

Then it takes anywhere from four days to a week for the penis to
heal
Subconsciously they really don't remember how that feels
But subconsciously most men wouldn't want to be tied down or
hand cuffed
Now fast-forward to manhood

When women go down on a man, we're simply apologizing for the
surgeons' behavior
We take our tongue and roll it up & down the shaft, take those
testicles
& let them float in our mouth like you're sitting in a tub of water
Then we take our tongue tip & lick around
That very rim that the surgeon made so perfect for us women to
enjoy

Then we suck & suck until cum run down the back of our throat or
down the sides of our mouth
That is the art to a circumcision

Beatitudes

Blessed are the poor in spirit, for theirs is the kingdom of heaven

    When my heart is lonely feeling of despair

    I shift my focus on my goal to heaven, I soon will be there

Blessed are they that mourn: for they shall be comforted

    Every time the world tries to do me harm

    Jesus comforts me by wrapping me in His arms

Blessed are the meek: for they shall inherit the earth

    Do not mistake my humbleness, sweetness, & meekness for weakness

    In the end I will shout because the world we see my sleekness

Blessed are they that hunger & thirst after righteousness; for they shall be filled

    It may appear that I don't have a life because I put God first

    Day in and day out the words of the Bible fills my soul & I no longer hunger or thirst

Blessed are the merciful for they shall obtain mercy

    It doesn't hurt to be kind doesn't cost a thing to smile

    For my brother & sister I will show love and walk the long mile

Blessed are the pure in heart, for they shall see God

    Wash me & I shall be whiter than snow

    Purge any evil thoughts or doings so close to God, I can grow

Blessed are the peacemakers, for they shall be called the children of God

    If I hold my peace & let the Lord fight my battles

    Victory shall be mines; I just need to avoid any hassles

Blessed are they which are persecuted for righteousness sake;

For theirs is the kingdom of heaven

    1, 2, 3, 4 – although we're talked about, ridiculed, put down, & considered a bore

    Continue to praise Him, He'll give you more

    4, 5, 6, 7 – I'm on my way to heaven

BIPOLAR LOVE

Baby I'm glad you're home
I love the flowers; they're so beautiful
Uumph! You smell so good – you know that's a turn on for me
I've got dinner ready for you. I'll just warm it up for you
I love you to death – you are God's gift to me
Sorry I missed your call earlier, I was in the shower
After dinner I'll give you a good massage
I can't wait to make love to you – imma put it down for you
I love you, come here & give me a hug

Humph! That was kind of a weak hug

What the fuck you get home so late for
You giving me these muthafuckn flowers like you're guilty or
something
Why you smelling so good? You musta showered while you were at
your heifers house
You might not wanna eat dinner – might be some mu'fuckn poison
in it
I tried to call you earlier & you didn't even answer
You ain't never did that bullshit before
You standing there with that stupid look on your face
You better not even be thinking about getting some bootie
Don't fucking touch me
Don't even watch me walk away
I hate you mufucka

BOX OF CHOCOLATES

Life is like a box of chocolates you never know what you're going to get

Love is like a box of chocolates you never know what you're going to get

Hate is like a box of chocolates you never know what you're going to get

Divorce is like a box of chocolates you never know what you're going to get

Sex is like a box of chocolates you never know what you're going to get

Poetry is like a box of chocolates you never know what you're going to get

A kiss is like a box of chocolates you never know what you're going to get

A touch is like a box of chocolates you never know what you're going to get

BOYFRIEND #1	BOYFRIEND #2
He likes my touch	he likes my kisses
He likes me in lace	he likes me in leather
He likes me as the French maid	he likes me as the naughty nurse
He likes it doggy style	he like it froggy style
He likes 68	he likes 69

They both like "1669"

He wants 3 children	he wants 2 & a dog
He wants me to meet his friends	he wants me to meet his parents
He wants to take me to St Martin	he wants to take me to Punta Cana
He calls my 1st name	he calls my 1st, middle, & last
He has mad luv	he has crazy luv

I enjoy both of them

He likes to video tape us	he likes mirrors
He likes fruit	he likes whip cream
He swallows me like reese' pieces	he likes the rim shot
He likes soft restraints	he likes the fuzzy cuffs
He likes fore play	he likes 12 play

They both wanna be with me

He likes to wear edible condoms	he likes edible body spray
He likes me in see thru boyshorts	he likes me in lace thongs
He like my nails air brushed	he likes my nails French tipped
He has natural talents with his tongue	he enhances with his tongue ring
He likes to spoon me	he likes for me to spoon him

I can't get enough of either of them

BUTTERFLY

Every night about 10 pm it's just me and my butterfly

I don't even fight the feeling anymore

Sometimes I just lay my butterfly next to me

or leave it under the pillow just in case I get the urge at 3 am

My butterfly stimulates my G-spot and my U-spot at the same time

Sometimes when I cum I squirt all over my hand, it feels like I wet myself

But I just produce large amounts of juice

CAN I LAY IN YOUR ARMS

Can I lay in Your arms
>Life can sometimes beat me til I'm broken
>Working hard every day to earn a piece of token

Can I lay in Your arms
>Slowful, depressed, self pity, just tired
>Searching months for a job for someone to say I'm hired

God can I lay in Your arms
>I need to get to You & be in your presence
>Cause when I'm weak, You're my strength

If I can just lay in Your arms
>I know everything will be ok
>Cause You've already made a way

Can I run into Your arms
>No one can love me like you do
>No one comfort & console me like you do

If I can just lay in Your arms
>As my passion for you grow strong
>Keep me from doing wrong

Can I lay in Your arms
>Cause satan is all around
>He keeps trying to level me to the ground

Father wrap me in Your arms
>Sometimes I win & sometimes I lose
>Sometimes I feel hurt & abused

Can I lay in Your arms
>When everything constantly attack me
>Being close to You, I know nothing can destroy me

Can I lay in Your arms
>Feeling lost when I go astray
>Even tho You give me instructions, I lost my way

Can I lay in Your arms

When this world is wicked sometimes
Every time I turn on the news, it blows my mind
Can I lay in Your arms
When I'm feeling lonely & deep in despair
Feeling like this world I can no longer bare

Can I lay in Your arms
When the enemy is pressing hard
I can speak over myself & encourage myself in the Lord

If I can just lay in Your arms
You're my rock, my source, my love, my strength
I can always run to you & repent

Can I lay in Your arms
Cause God You're the joy & the strength of my life
You move all pain, misery, & strife

Can I lay in Your arms
You promised to keep me – never to leave me
You've never ever come short of Your word

Can I lay in Your arms
You're a wheel in the middle of a wheel, a way otta no way
Protector, healer, comforter day by day

In Your arms there's peace –In Your arms there's mercy
In Your arms there's grace – In Your arms there's love
In Your arms there's power – In Your arms there's redemption
In Your arms there's favor – In Your arms there's rest
In Your arms there's protection – In Your arms there's rejuvenation
In Your arms there's kindness – In Your arms there's forgiveness

So Father, can I lay in Your arms

CRUSH

I've been walking pass him like he don't even see me
All along those eyes were following me
Somehow he was smitten by me
But me being so much older, huh, this just can't be

I try to tell myself "t you'll get over it, be resistible"
But I can't act like his fine ass is invisible
With his sexy voice & his slender body, oh my, what is this?!
Help me please I need to resist

Every time I see him I have to touch his hand
He squeezes a lil bit to let me know he is a man
Oowwee, I better watch out, if I let him, I know he can
Turn me inside out, upside down, maybe even a handstand

Wish I could shake him maybe he'll go away
It will be just as hard tomorrow as it was today
Myself try to tell me, "gurl walk the otha way"
But instead I walk over & say ....."HEY"

DEM BONES

Singing ♫ "dry bones, dry bones, dry bones, drryyyyyy bones"
"dry bones, dry bones, dry bones, drryyyyyy bones"
Anybody want some dryyy bones??

Dem bones be coming to church talking bout this, talking bout that, talking talking talking but ain't saying nothing
Hyssop, gossiping, spreading rumors, talking nonsense, going off, always stirring up something
They don't have understanding, no peace, can't get the word, don't know what they done heard
Always barking...................................that's dem dog bones

Dem bones don't help axillaries. They Sunday morning members; therefore, the word comes & the word goes.
Don't encourage others, can't minister cause the word has no foundation, it's gone before they get home
Can't have the brother or sister's back cause they not strong. But they sholl come dressed up real nice from head to
toe..that's dem weak bones

Dem bones look like a devout Christian, always praising God, look like they doing His will
Look holy, speak holy, walk holy, dressed holy, singing holy. Uump, when they around other church folk.
But, sounding as a loud cymbal. they don't have God, it means nothing...that's dem broke bones

Dem bones clean on the inside, clean on the outside; fresh as an ice cream paint job
They work hard in the church and work hard in the community. They love serving God.
They are prayer warriors, set good examples; they're about God's business, they worship Him relentless.
They're like the church of
Philadephia..................................that's dem strong bones

Dem bones sit on the bench, they don't praise, don't wave their hand, don't pat their feet,

Stoned faced, no smile. But after church during fellowship, they 1st in line when it's time to eat
They hear the word but don't apply it to life. Walking around with bitterness & strife
head hanging low…………………………….that's dem dry bones

"….prophesy upon these bones, and say unto them, o ye dry bones, hear the word of the Lord. Thus saith the Lord God unto these bones; behold, I will cause breath to enter into you, and ye shall live"
Ezekiel 37: 4 & 5

Singing 🎵 "dry bones, dry bones, dry bones, drryyyyyy bones"
"dry bones, dry bones, dry bones, drryyyyyy bones"
Anybody want some dryyy bones??

DESIRE

MY FINE CHOCOLATE BROTHER
I WONDER IF HE KNOWS I HAVE PASSION FOR HIM LIKE NO
OTHER
I TRY TO UNDERSTAND WHY IT RUNS DEEP THROUGH ME
IT FEELS WIDER & DEEPER THAN ANY SEA
WHY DO I HAVE A DESIRE FOR ANOTHER LADY'S MAN?
IT CREEPS THROUGH MY BONES LIKE FIRE
A STRONG DESIRE TO FEEL HIS TOUCH
A STRONG DESIRE TO HEAR HIS VOICE
A STRONG DESIRE TO BE CLOSE TO HIM
HOLD HIM, FEEL HIM, AND TASTE HIM
I KNOW THIS SITUATION IS WRONG
I DON'T EVEN WANT TO REMAIN STRONG
I'M DRIVING MYSELF RIGHT INTO TEMPTATION
ALL ALONG I'M CONTEMPLATING
SHOULD I STAY OR SHOULD I GO
SOMEBODY HELP ME 'CAUSE I DON'T KNOW

DID YOU GET FULLY DRESSED TODAY?

And why should we wear the whole armor?
…..to protect ourselves from the whiles of the prince of darkness.

Put the helmet of salvation on your head
To rebuke foul & ugly words that could be said
To rebuke thoughts and actions not of Him
Be ye alert and stay prayerful & meditate on God's grace and His
kingdom which is our goal

Put on the breast plate of righteousness
To be guarded against lust
Protect your heart against hatred, revenge, bitterness
So your heart can love pure & unconditional

Wear the belt of truth around your waist
To show that we are ambassadors of Jesus Christ

Be sure your feet are fitted with the right shoes, least you trip over
your own two feet.
Your feet have significance in the balance of your entire body.
If the soles of your shoes are not sealed with the gospel of peace
You will run into: brick walls, u turns, confusions, & wars you cannot
fight
The gospel of peace will make you ready & you will be able to stand
firm

Don't forget to bring the shield of faith
That shield will guard against: temptation, going the broad road,
weaknesses, doubt
That shield will guard against: being lukewarm & other tricks of the
wicked one
Our faith in the Trinity, our faith in our Christian walk, our faith in the
New Jerusalem is embedded in our shield

But most of all hold the sword of the Spirit, which is the word of God

The wicked one is looking for you to be undressed so he can plan his
attack
So put on the whole armor and go fearlessly in the world
Put on the whole armor to be warriors for Christ
Put on the whole armor because our struggle is not of the flesh only
but of rulers of evil

DON'T DO GOD NO FAVORS

Com'mon let's go to church; all week u been at school & work
Look at sis so'nso coming in late. Walking down the middle isle like a
superstar.
With those fancy shoes & fancy purse.
All heads turning, while u causing a distraction
Yeah, u aint' supposed to be shining, it's about God.

Deacons trying to pray while u checking ur text message
Can't even give the preacher a minute of ur time, how u gon get the
message.
Oh, I c, God on yo time....u ain't on God's time....i thought God own
the time
Then time after time...u going thru the motions.

U paid ur do's by coming to church for a couple hours
But u couldn't get the word rooted so the rest of the week ur
devoured
Cuz satan keeps u in yo reprobated mind; U carrying spirits of all
kinds
Leave those spirits behind; drop those spirits of on the parking lot.
Try not to look back like Lots wife's did

Better yet, learn how to purge. So ppl can see the God in u
Not a hell raiser...doing what u always do...do u
Learn that phrase. Doing u, is not doing God
Consume the preachers word so u can make God proud
Spread of His goodness spread of his word

How can they see the God in u when u always frowning, always down,
always sad
Always cussing, always fussing, always arguing, always mad
Make satan mad by always smiling, always witnessing, always praising
The more u get the word, the more u purge of yourself

DON'T SWALLOW

I know you want me to sit on your face
You're so excited you can't wait to taste
But I must warn you before hand
'Cause once you get started, you won't stand a chance
See I know what you're thinking,
You're anxious to get a hold of me
Can't wait to have me fiending & sprung for you
You just want me to relax & let you do what you do

So I straddle you, mound you like I'm about to experience
almond joy
You grab hold of my hips like I'm your favorite toy
My thighs wrap around both your ears
My thoughts confusing as I embrace my fears
You kiss gently to tease me right quick
I reach back and take hold of your d--k
I take my thumb & rub the wetness from you pre-cum
Then you take your tongue & lips & give me more
You put your tongue tip on my clit
Started kissing around my lips
I tried to run – but for you that was fun
You weren't having that, you held me tight,
I tried to resist with all my might

You sucked & licked & I came & squirt
Trying to maintain but again & again I burst
I tried to tap out cause I couldn't take it no more
But you was sopping like it was your greatest adore
I said 'baby please' you should probably stop
You kept going, owee, imma pop
Baby stop! Don't swallow, it's not good for your mental
health
If you swallow it, you gon be mad at yourself
But he kept going, driving me insane
All the nerve synapses separated in my brain
I could no longer maintain

My body jerked, I almost gave myself whiplash
He just worked that tongue faster & faster
He held on tight & I couldn't fight
Shock waves shot through my body while my heart was racing
But he held steady with his tongue fast pacing
"baby, im about to max out! Please don't swallow"
I'm trushing & rocking & screaming & making high pitched sounds

His ass swallowed, & instead of getting me sprung
He wanted more of my juices
He drank me all up & wanted to drink more
He keeps calling me back for more
I got fifty messages in an hour with him begging
So I finally call him & told him he was warned not to swallow
He said he never tasted sweet nectar & he couldn't get enough
He can't eat, can't sleep, can't focus, but he wants to drink me again
How do I detox this man? I mean, it was only once
But I did say, "don't swallow"

DOWN ON ME

You did something so beautiful and extreme
Let me try to explain what I mean
    You went down on me trying to find my pearl treasure
    Then you gave me a rush of unbelievable pleasure
        You swallowed me like reese' pieces
        You licked, you sucked, you kissed – all three great
        teases
            You had all my juices on a consistent flow,
            Whether I'm going or coming, I still don't
            know

You flipped me, sucked me, licked me more
And although I wanted you to stick me
    You held me, gripped me & wouldn't let go
    I still didn't know if I was coming or going
        Then more screams of passion, moans, shrieks &
        high pitches
        Sounds of love definitely being made
            My mind was gone; I lost control, my toes
            curled
            Then I had the best climax in the world

For you to claim to be an amateur, I couldn't tell
Cause you did it mighty mighty well
    You made love to me in a different way
    Had me trippin for the rest of the day
        I was walking around in such a daze
        Couldn't get over the complex amaze
            I'm so glad you didn't let go until I came
            You made love to me – it was no game

ESPECIALLY DIFFERENT

He looks at me as if he's studying what to say
Looks at me like he has a crush on me
But I can feel in his soul he thinks he loves me
He stares when he thinks I'm not looking
He watches the sweetness of my walk
It's hard for him to look me in the eye
He falls for my smile every time, like it's just for him
My mere presence heals him
He thinks he can have me & he wants to make me happy
He daydreams about me
He wants to embrace me & not let me go
Whatever chance he gets to spend with me he'll take
Most men would leave or let go
That's how I know, he loves me especially different

FANTASY WORLD

Both of us have our situation; I know it's not easy
    When I look in your eyes almost instantly
Pain in my heart is set free
    I know you can love the hurt away
All you have to do is stay
    Will I ever love again – could you change my mind?
We could miss an opportunity for what our hearts can't find
    I'm talking about a love high that's so divine
Seems like we've been friends for a long while
    When I look at you I can always see a sparkle in your smile
You give me a joy that feels so pure
    I get scared sometimes, but my hearts' secure
Are you going to turn away from your hearts' desire?
    Do you think you're playing with fire?
Can I be the treasure in your heart?
    Baby don't you know, when we're apart…
Someone's with me but I feel alone
    Longing to hear your voice on the phone
Sweet as morning dew
    I can't wait to get next to you
Look at your body like the moonlight
    Just too much for me to fight
I've noticed sometimes when you're in my arms
    You can get weakened by my charms
Or are you messing with my feelings?
    Tempted by the love that's forbidden?
Do you know you have precious love that my heart beats for?
    Why do you think I keep knocking at your door?
Like a junkie for love you got me fiending
    When I think about you – talk to you – with you, I'm
    always beaming
When I look in your eyes
    I get a natural high
When I'm close to you all I can see
    Is that you make me weak in the knees
Letting me love you in places no one's' found
    Doctor, you better chill
Your love's making me ill

You make my river overflow
Bring out an inner glow
Heaven's far away but you can bring it right here
You make my soul whole so kind & dear
You measure up in size
You can satisfy
I get high so high
You may be over qualified
I know what the burning in our hearts could be
Because of our situation, it won't be easy

FROM A KING TO A QUEEN

I be missn u so much – I never had quite the lust
When I'm at work, I can't get my mind off u
Keep looking at the clock like – dang 8 mo hrs til I get back to u
Yes, I no I used to b obsessed with my king
He did me so rite, especially at nite with no lites
Sorry I had to let him go, I just needed a change
He was jus a lil too big & hard to maintain

But u r beautiful – a pleasure 2c
Musta been sent from heaven exclusively 4me
But now that I have u its so amazing
When we're together I'm blazen & glazen
How can I not think about when we were last 2gether
U always give me great pleasure
It's a shame I had to choose between him & her
My king or my queen – don't wanna make it seem
Like I'm mean, but out with the king & in with the queen

When I get off work, I speed down the highway 2get 2u
Pull up in the driveway, run thru the door to get 2u
Throw my keys somewhere, strip while I'm running down the hall 2
u
Finally, I get to u & I jump all ova u
Roll around in u as I was lusting for u all day

Spread eagle in my 820 thread counted sheets
While my queen is made to fit me
My queen is a 4post cherry canopy
That treats me like the queen of Sheba
Serta mattress with memory foam built to fit my curves
So screw that king – I got my queen!

FUCK YOU VERY MUCH

For luring me in so sweet romantic & innocently
But a wolf in sheep clothing is all you turned out to be

FUCK YOU VERY MUCH
For selling your house moving in with me, say'n you're gon
pay off your bills then help me with mine
But every time we went out, I had to pay for the movies and
wine & dine

FUCK YOU VERY MUCH
For being 43yrs old hiding under the bed for an hour, like it
was a joke
Never giving me a dime on a $1000 house note

FUCK YOU VERY MUCH
For saying we're one, you're the head of the house, I'm
supposed to b submissive
But every time I was gone leave the house I had to ask your
permission?

FUCK YOU VERY MUCH
For tryna tell me when I can & can't talk, what I can & can't
wear
Who I can & can't have as a friend & how I should do my hair

FUCK YOU VERY MUCH
For acting like a perfect couple when we're n public like I'm
your trophy
But behind closed doors – it was sleeping with the enemy

FUCK YOU VERY MUCH
While I was at work you went thru things of mine
Then when I got home u wanna be in my face wasting my
time

FUCK YOU VERY MUCH
When my motor burnt out my dad gave me another, but to
get it I had to catch the bus to Chicago
When in our driveway we had a scooter, Chevy pickup, a
Malibu & a Camaro

FUCK YOU VERY MUCH

36

For stealing my skates so I couldn't go to skate king
And for all these things you want me to treat you like my king

FUCK YOU VERY MUCH
For all the good good that you got got that had you in seizures
of epileptic
Each time you got it your body was in motions of tonic and
colonic

FUCK YOU VERY MUCH
The more I gave you the more your mind was gone
Took all my keys to the house and car and held me captive in
my own home

FUCK YOU VERY MUCH
For telling me I can't write a book, then taking & hiding my
poetry
Maaann, you're messing with my love, my heart, my soul —
the essence of me

FUCK YOU VERY MUCH
For each time u said u were gonna get counseling so for the
next 100 yrs u & I can work
Each time I let my guards down, all I did was get hurt

FUCK YOU VERY MUCH
For cut'n my furnace & put'n a bag of sugar in my gas tank
Tryna act like some neighborhood kids were pulling a prank

FUCK YOU VERY MUCH
For forcing yourself on me with a smile on your face
I said no at least 15 times, that wasn't love, that was a
disgrace

FUCK YOU VERY MUCH
For the restraining order I got on you & if I ever see you any
time soon
I will cut your testicles off & put 'em in some formaldehyde

FUCK YOU VERY MUCH
Yes I had a lil attitude when I wrote this poem so if you don't
like it

FUCK YOU VERY MUCH

FUQUE LUV SON

his a$$ broke into my heart again. but he's no ordianary burgular. he keeps coming back. and i allow him. i'm so stupid to keep falling for him & his okie doke. wish i cud call 5-0 so they cud lock him up. but they dont wanna be bothered with me talkn bout i cry wolf, imma just let him back in - again and again. but i do kick him out, but 5-0 is right - i let him back in time & time again. he makes me happy, he makes me sad, he makes me cry, he makes me mad, he makes me fiend for it, make my heart ache for it, he confuse me. he scares me. i keep saying imma be strong next time but again i lied. oh how i want to die. he keeps playing with me. he acts like he is for real each time. keeps blowing my mind. he sweeps me off my feet with his charm. but he cause me to have anxiety, mixed emotions in me, feel like i wanna scream. i toss and turn have restless nights. i'm fragile and he doesn't seem to care. he take my trust for granted. he just comes after me whenever he feels like it. like he's preys on me. he takes love & gives love he thinks I need. he knows he's my weakness....HIS NAME IS LOVE ....

FUQUE LUV SON!!

Good Friends Have Your Back

In kindergarten a little girl was picking on me because my eyes were bubbled,
my nose was fat my lips were thick, & my hair was kinky.
When I got home I was crying in my room and didn't want no body to
see me. My friend came over & asked why I won't come out to play.
I told her what happened & the next day I went to school that lil girl
was bald headed. I didn't know whether to ask what happened or laugh
but that girl never said another word to me & her hair never did grow back.

When I was in 7th grade, sitting in the class room, a boy kept poking his finger in the
back of my head while the rest of the class laughed.
I asked him over and over again to leave me alone – then there I go again, crying.
My friend said somebody been messing with you again? I told her what happened.
When I went back to school, I didn't see that boy for two weeks.
When he came back to school, his hand & arm were in a cast
Finally, I caught up with him in the hall & asked what happened
but soon as he saw my friend he just walked the other way.

When I was senior in high school, my boyfriend was a freshman in college.
I wanted to wait until I was married. He said it was ok. Me and my friend went to see
him for spring break and I caught him humping some chic. I ran back to the car crying
and my friend asked me what happened. After I told her, she said she'd be right back.
She went in her trunk and ran into the dorm while she was on her cell phone. When she
came back, she had a black plastic bag wrapped real tight.
At the same time the ambulance pulled up. We were about to drive back to St Louis.
About half way over a bridge, she stopped the car, got out, opened the bag, put a big
rock in it, and threw it over into the Mississippi.

When I was 25, I was engaged. My fiancé had a bachelor's party the day before the
wedding. I asked the housekeeper for a key because I'd lost mine. I crept in the room at
2am while he was passed out with two women laid up with him passed out as well. I went
back home call my friend and couldn't talk from being choked up on emotions. I told her
what happened. The next day she convinced me to go to the wedding because it would
never happen again. So, later that evening, I was stood up at the altar.
Even now, some years later, his best man, his friends, his mom & dad, even the police
can't find his body or a trace of him.

When I was 40, I couldn't take it anymore. I called my best friend in Atlanta and asked her what happened to all those people.

1) The little girl in kindergarten was seduced by my friend into washing her hair with something special so it would grow long like Raponzel. That little girl got her hair washed in draino, bleach, and hair relaxer with lye

2) That 7th grade boy who was poking me in my head got his finger tips chopped up in a grinder because my friend asked him to reach in there to get the diamond. If he gets it, he could have it.

3) My college boyfriend was castrated from the base of his penis. My friend was calling the ambulance on her way into the dorm and his penis was in the plastic bag when she threw it into the Mississippi.

4) My fiancé who broke my heart laying up in bed with two women, well, he disappeared "without a trace"....thanks to my friend.

So I guess that's what good friends do. Good friends have your back.

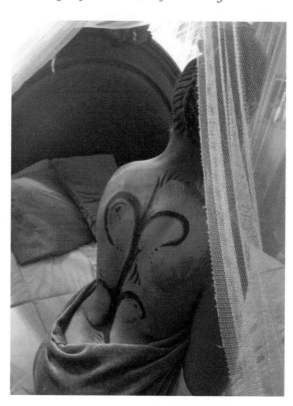

GREAT PLEASURE

I made love to you in a different kind of way
What a lovely ending to my day

I touched you with the base of my hands to my finger tips
From your neck to your ankles including your hip

I touched, rubbed you massaged & caressed you
Sculptured your body wishing you were my boo

Massaging your thighs made my temperature rise
Just for our skin to touch, put me on natural highs

As I pressed my breast against your back
I rested my pubic area between your crack

Then as you came in my hand I had to catch my drool
Glad I had my panties on to catch my pool

I could smell your sweetness when you came
For me to hold back caused me torturous pain

You shared just a small piece of your treasure
Your nut you had, gave me great pleasure

HAIKU & SHORT POEMS

Can you please love me
Simply not forever complex
Love, simplexity

'Spose to rain today
I got a burst of sun ray
What a summer day

Ejaculations
Go where, gaze up on the ceiling
And see it there

Imma beast all I wanna do
Is have a feast, don't forget add yeast
To my bread in the east

Love my president is black
As the sea on a midnight ride
To the grocery store for milk

What you need, you desire
24-7, 365, stalker-ish

You are blessed and highly favored
Know that, believe that, & live that
Because God is that & Jesus his Son
Died so you & I could have life & live that

I feel so close to you, you're a
String bean & imma bean in your pod

For you in the dark shadows of
The room I saw the sparkle in your
Eyes & the smile upon your lips
Listened to the song in your heart

Breathe in deeply of each new
Day, cause love is always
A heart-beat away

Your chocolate can melt
In my mouth not in my hand
Unless you want

sky is in the sky
the reason why it's high
the ocean is low why

I don't work well under
pressure measure the texture
of my pleasure

try to walk between the
raindrops in case of a surprise
thunderstorm

my last two dollars, im not
gonna loose; got one for my jukebox
other one for my bus fair

the room is dark & gloomy
wondering who hand is that touching
me
I turn look see, it's me

sweet dreams my love hope you
had a blessed day & even more
Blessed & highly favored tomorrow

making love to you on a mountain
top listening to our echoes of
sounds, screams & love moans

just thinking bout you cause
rainy days & Thursdays always
Make me wet

you water me with life & feed me
see, your sunshine – together life is oh
so fine

donuts remind me of me
you can eat them from the
front or the back

I love the sound of flip flop
thong shoes, reminds me of
bootie clapping

HE

He came into my heart like a quiet storm with his brown
skin & laid back subtle exterior.He invited me into his
space, & I, he, into mine. B4i knew it, into the bedroom
we lye.He absorbs & consumes my mind...my thoughts,
my brain. I'm going insane
Cause he is guarded and distant & has stipulations: but
I can't comprehend the fornications.I won't separate my
love from my lust because together they spontaneously
bust.How else cud one explain waking up at 3am at the
height of a climax?Cause he deep within me
subconsciously won't allow me to relax
I want all of he not some of he I want to be we
But he doesn't know cause he has an hiatus and again
I'm lonely

So when he with his mocha colored skin calls me
He easily slips into the vulnerable parts of my heart
that awaits another.And he misses me & he wants to be
with me.And he wants me to say his name & the more I
said his name.The more intense the flick of his tongue
became & I came.And he erased the pain that was
stained from the brown skin he.But he cud not maintain
so again I remain → lonely.Cause the brown skin he
spoiled me but he did not try to .He just likes me &
enjoys being with me from time, but he won't allow his
mind.To have all of me - but he sure likes some of me

Then he with his chocolate colored skin was instantly
seduced by my invitation.And he lay with me, and he
smelled the pear glaze˙ from my Victoria secret
It smelled good so it must taste good. He inhaled me & I
exhaled him.He received the pleasure from the passion
that was misplaced.Not in good taste but still felt great.
And his chocolate melted in my mouth not in my hands.
just like m&m candies, he definitely came in handy.But
like a full coarse meal, he cleaned his plate as I sat on
his face.But it's he & he & he & they want she which is
me, but my soul is scattered because of he

HE GIVES ME FEVER

The song says it best...."you give me fever"
When I see you coming walking toward me
My body temperature rises a few degrees
I see you & within just a few feet
My temperature rises even more degrees
I hear your voice
Again my temperature rises
I anticipate the next time I will see you
My temperature rises
I dream about you to the point that makes me climax
"What a lovely way to burn!"
My hands get sweaty my body breaks out in a sweat
You can call it Fahrenheit or Centigrade
Either way, I feel like I'm on fire
He gives me fever

HEALING ME

His positive words heal me
The sound of his voice heals me
His passionate kiss heals me
The warmth of his embrace heals me
His hands thru my hair heals me
His compliments heals me
The way he laughs heals me
His smile heals me
The depth of his emotions heals me

HOMELESS SPIRITS OF GOD

The spirit of God keeps trying to get in but we won't allow Him

Because of our ignorance.

We're walking around high & mighty, holier than thou

Like we aint never done no wrong

But deep within, we harbor: fornication, idolatry, bitterness, pride, grudges, jealousy, enviousness, strife, trifle, backbiting, controlling, manipulative behavior, adultery, deceptive behavior, cheating, slowfulness, selfishness, drunkenness, defiling our bodies, lasciviousness

It's no wonder why we got heavy loads.

All these spirits we harbor, occupies too much space so there's no room for God's spirit to dwell.

We need to shake off some of that dead weight, if not all.

Or, else God's spirits will continue to roam & knock trying to get in

But until then, the good spirits will remain, homeless

HOPELESS CASE

What's up Mr Brown skin
      U wanna replenish my faith in men?
            I once had a love so great
                  Thought I'd found my soul mate

But he taught me how a heart could break
      I learned 1st hand about the thin line between love & hate
            Then I couldn't stand for a man to being in my face
                  I blocked the world out & found my own
                  space

Then along came you with your hidden charm
      Acting as my protector – like you'd do me no harm
            Did God send me my Mr Right?
                  Someone I can hold close every night?

He wants to fix this crack in my heart
      So strong that nothing will keep us apart
            He knows what to do when I flip my mood
                  He keeps his cool- not act a fool

He gets in where he fits in
      Already sprung on this nice size ten
            No doubt he's playing for keeps
                  Just a matter of time before he falls too deep

I can't fall in love 'cause I'm saving it all for me
      Cause for right now that's the way it has to be
            But I love how he lights up when he see my face
                Even though, I'm a hopeless case

I AM A CHRISTIAN

I AM CHRISTIAN, HOWEVER, THAT IS A PART OF ME, I AM ALSO SINGLE, SEXY, CELIBATE, WOMAN, MOTHER, NURSE, DANCER, NURTURER, HONEST, WEAR MY FEELINGS ON MY SLEEVE, SENSITIVE BUT STRONG, INTELLIGENT, BEAUTIFUL ON THE INSIDE THAT MANIFEST ON THE OUTSIDE, I'M A SHOULDER, POET, WRITER, READER, EDUCATOR, AUNT, SISTER, DAUGHTER, PHILOSOPHER, JOKESTER, SWEET, NEAT FREAK, DISCOMBOBULATED, COMPOSED, RESERVE, CRAZY, I HAVE SEX APPEAL, I'M AN AWESOME & GREAT LOVER (THAT'S WHAT I HEARD)..... AT TIMES I CAN BE COLD, DISTANT, HAPPY THEN SAD. HATE YOU LIKE POISON & LOVE YOU MAD. SOMETIMES ALL TOGETHER SOMETIMES SEPARATE ~ DON'T JUDGE ME OR HATE ON ME...JUST LOVE ME

I APOLOGIZE TO MY KING

I was a queen – well at least a human being
Til I was ripped from my homeland – the only place I've ever
known
The ship was a long, three month ride of hatred, abuse, and
constant rape
The smell was nauseating and you could smell us miles away
We were sleeping in own urine, laying so close to one another
While feces spewed onto the next slave

When we hit land, I heard the bids for us
Forced to do as they say, their rules, their lives, their names
We were equal to or less than their animals – NOT REAL PEOPLE
I may be a Jones but deep down I'm: izzie, Kenya, kisobo, ibo, tobie

They took us, defiled us, polluted us with their seeds
Creating what they called pick-a-ninnies
They snuck out in the middle of the night from their precious
white pearls
Violated us even the night before our weddings
Sometimes it felt as massa was pissing inside of us
But other times, massa had everything to prove to our husbands;
So he raped us gently & we had no choice but to reflexively get wet
and enjoy him.

Our husbands started to resent us because he knew when he had to come behind massa
But worse of all our husbands resented themselves for not being strong enough for his wife & children to protect them.

But the story doesn't end there

Some men were bought by other men to hide their abomination →
molly's they call them
The man was married to their pearl of a woman but raping & training our bucks

Sometimes the white woman would got tired of all the secrecy
They began to force our bucks to have sex with them.
If he said no, she'd yell rape & he's put to death in the worse way
(by cutting off his penis, shove it in his mouth & hanged from a noose on a tree
Then set on fire "ALIVE")
But when she was caught or became pregnant, she still yelled rape
– and he, my king was still put to death

AND FOR THESE THINGS, I APOLOGIZE TO MY KING

I GRIEVE

*I missed you from the very first moment I heard your heart
beat
In my belly life given, only about five or six weeks
I missed your eyes, your fingers; wish I could've kissed your
tiny little feet
I guess you weren't meant for me to keep
Even years later I grieve my abortion; yes, I still weep
If I make it to heaven, I look forward to when we meet*

I JUST WANNA PRAISE HIM

My heart is filled with praise
I just wanna praise Him
If thou w/draw thy hand from me where will I go
I just wanna praise Him
He woke me up this morning
I just wanna praise Him
You gave Your life on Calvary
I just wanna praise Him
I coulda been eatin fruitloops
I just wanna praise Him
While coocoo for coco puffs
I just wanna praise Him
I lift you up, I magnify Your name
I just wanna praise Him
He clothed me in my right mind
I just wanna praise Him
When the weight of the world is on my shoulder
I just wanna praise Him
Sometimes I'm tossed & driven
I just wanna praise Him
'Cause You kept me so I won't let go
I just wanna praise Him
I'm battered by an angry sea
I just wanna praise Him
When Im happy
I just wanna praise Him
I wanna sing praises
I just wanna praise Him
When the storms of life are raging
I just wanna praise Him
When I'm sad, I will yet praise Him
I just wanna praise Him
When His Spirit falls on me
I just wanna praise Him
When praises go up blessings come down
I just wanna praise Him
He's given me so many gifts
I just wanna praise Him
When I'm smiling thru my tears

I just wanna praise Him
He brings me thru my trials & tribulations
I just wanna praise Him
You gave us Your only Son
I just wanna praise Him
He never left me alone
I just wanna praise Him
I plead the Blood of Jesus
I just wanna praise Him
I don't want the rocks to cry out for me
I just wanna praise Him
You let me see a brand new day
I just wanna praise Him
I want to shout of Your excellence
I just wanna praise Him
Even at my lowest
I just wanna praise Him
He heard my cry & pitied every grown
I just wanna praise Him
When He increase me
I just wanna praise Him
Father I stretch my hand to thee
I just wanna praise Him
Thru the rain thru the pain
I just wanna praise Him
Thru sunny days & rainy days
I just wanna praise Him
I don't know about luck but I know I'm blessed
I just wanna praise Him
He's been mighty mighty mighy good to me
I just wanna praise Him
When doctors say no, You say yes
I just wanna praise Him
I'm greatful so greatful so greatful
I just wanna praise Him
With my whole heart, whole mind & whole body
I just wanna praise Him

If I had 10,000 tongues ~ I could not praise Him enough!!

55

I LOVE MY BROTHA'S

I love my brothas, chocolate brothas, moco & coco colored brothas
High yellow & twinkie colored brothas, peanut butta & caramel colored bothas
Lite bright near white looking brothas, brothas from another motha.
Dem whining & crying brothas, articulate brothas, quiet & talkative brothas
But especially the ones who love, respect,
& take care of their children & mothers, brotha

I love my brothas tall brothas, short brothas, fat brothas
Double wide brothas, thick brothas, thin brothas, muscle bound brothas
Or long as they can hold me against the wall brotha
Ball head brothas, hair locked up brothas, faded & clean cut brothas,
Good haired brothas, braided brothas, young & old brothas
But if you gon step to me please be older than 40 brotha

I luv my brothas, sweet talking brothas, long winded brothas
God fearing brothas, deep voice brothas, deep stroking brothas
Good singing brothas, musically inclined brothas
Affectionate brothas, exploratory brothas, intelligent brothas
Nosey ass brothas, curious brothas
Talkn smack like he's hard, but weak to my sistas type of brotha

I love my brothas ⇑ hard headed brothas & ⇓ hard headed brothas
Fix my car 4me brotha, cook for me every now and then brotha
Feed me cuz that's my aphrodisiac brotha, rub my feet for me brotha
Uniform wearing brothas, poetic brothas, blue & white collared brothas
Long as u have a job brotha
& of coarse my three favorite T's on a brotha
Good teeth, nice toes, & non hairy testicles on a brotha

If I were the wind

If I was the wind
I'd float through the atmosphere
I'd blow up a few dresses
I'd blow off a few hats
I'd blow a few leaves
I'd blow in your ear
I'd cool you when you're gardening
I'd breathe on you when you're laying in your hammock
I'll make the smoke from your incent float in the air & the motions from the curve of your
bodies making love & will reshape the rhythm of the flow
I'd just float free as a bird that was caged now with no worries
I'd travel the four corners of the earth

I'm Falling In Sprung

His touch, sends shocks & waves of electricity that shuts up in my bones
His passion makes me weak in the knees, 'cause he rights all my past wrongs
> God has sent me someone special — no more waiting & yearning & hoping
> Since he's here, I have no more sadness & whining & moping
He has broken thru chains, padlocks, 3 layers of bricks thicker than the walls of
Jericho
Have me doing things out the ordinary — can't say no — then I'm fiending for some
mo
> My climax no longer wants to be alone because his ejaculations have become
> my reliance
> Rather my thighs wrapped around his neck or hips or my ankles above his
> head, My body is in total compliance

The words uttered from his mouth is trustworthy, it's in the reliability of his
rhetoric's
Making love echoes, moans, those 3 syllables, become more powerful than musical
lyrics
> He ask if he can come over, I say no, he says baby please, I say yeah
> He knows I can't resist him — what the hell
My eardrums catches his words then rings thru my head vibrates ripples doubles then
triples
Keep traveling down my spinal cord til it bifurcates the split it hits my clit & tickles
> Moco/coco against my caramel is the make up of our complexed skin
> Once he gets to rubbing & caressing, I can't help but to give in

When I'm wrapped up in his arms, nothing else exist, time stands still
Time becomes timeless, seconds secondless, time is gone, I'm at his becking will
> Although I have insecurities about my stretch-marks & hysterectomy scars
> He makes me feel beautiful & sexy — like I'm perfect even in my flaws
His lips become glued then unglued to various parts of my body
Putting his tongue here & there has become his favorite hobby
> When his hands & fingers begin to tease my clitoris, my legs spread
> reflexively
> As I lay on my back, cum has already ran down my ass crack for him
> exclusively

He even makes love to my pubic hairs with his finger tips
He explores somewhere in the middle til he gets to the split of my lips
>> Deep penetrations, sometimes together masturbation, no more abstaination
>> His gifts to me, several multiples of five and orgasm, shit! What jubilation
He be slapping my ass like "go ahead get it girl get it girl"
damn! That man know he be rocking my world
>> I be tryna tap out like one two three
>> I'm tired & dehydrated it's his turn to get on top of me

Going round for round, pound for pound, my king has the strength of superiority
The blessings of fatiqueness has made me too tired in my inferiority
>> When he gets his 1st nut, I say ooh, happy valentine's day
>> By the time he gets his 2nd, I'm feeling like it's Christmas day
He can't help but to watch me walk away several times a day; he's instantly hypnotized
I can see the love & the lust in his eyes that seduces me into becoming mesmerized
>> To resist this man's love to rebel against God's blessing would be an onus
>> So instead I SUBMIT to my weakness, I'm sprung — it's actually my bonus

I'M IN LOVE WITH A MAN – NOT YOUR ORDINARY LOVE LETTER

I'm in love with a Man. And this is no ordinary Man. And this Man has no ordinary love.
His love is powerful & strong – unique and oh so sweet.
Sometimes when I lay in bed, I can feel Him gently wrap His arms around me.
And if my tears begin to flow, He wipes them all away.
And if He chooses to wake me in the morning, I know its gon be a brighter day.

He knows every hair on my head. And He knows where I am at all times.
He's jealous, but He's not obsessed. He just wants all of my love and all of my attention.
He loves me so much He will be whatever I need Him to be. He has several degrees –
Doctor, lawyer, counselor, & if I could create a degree, I'd call Him quite wonderful.

I daydream about Him or should I say meditate on Him day & night –
Of His goodness, and His sweetness, and His unconditional love –
That type of love that binds me with His Father
He doesn't ask for much from me but my faithfulness, loyalty, walk in His ways, daily devotions, talk to Him from time to time, introduce Him to my friends, and cleave unto Him.

This man takes care of me. He feeds me, gives me clothes. He even pays my house note.
Although He doesn't carry a 9mm, or brass knuckles, he protects me & watches over me, and His blood covers me.
As Song of Solomon says, "when He kisses me with the kisses of His mouth, His love is sweeter than wine." One touch form Him, oh, sends chills through my spine.
I say it's just like fire – shut up in my bones; much better than that love jones.
I've always got a song in my heart because He makes me so happy.
Cain't no body do me like Him!

He loves me more than Adam loved Eve. More than Abraham loved Isaac as he was about to give him as a burnt offering.
More than the love that caused Leah's affliction over Jacob.
More than the seven years Jacob served to obtain & marry Rachel.
Especially more than the dedication & commitment Ruth had for her mother in law Naomi.

More passionate than when David laid his eyes on Bathsheba & definitely more than the lengths David went through to get Bathsheba.
He loves me more than all the women who love Solomon.
More than King Ahauerus was mesmerized by Queen Esther.
He loves me more than the disciple who they say He loved.

Nothing will ever come between me & my love for Him.
Not death nor life, nor angels or principalities, or powers, nor things present, nor things to come, nor height or depth or any other creature.
And I love Him with all my heart & all my soul & all my might!
Surely I am in love.

I'M OBSESSED, THEREFORE I WILL STALK YOU THEN FALL IN LOVE WITH YOU

I DON'T WANT YOU TO THINK I WANT YOU
DON'T WANT YOU TO THINK I DESIRE YOU
I DON'T REALLY KNOW YOU; I JUST WANT TO STALK
YOU
AS I STALK YOU – I WILL GET TO KNOW YOU
WORK YOUR NERVES SO BAD YOU WILL DOUBLE GUESS
YOURSELF
I DREAM & DAYDREAM AND THINK ABOUT BEING
OBSESSED WITH YOU
I WILL SIT OUTSIDE OF YOUR HOUSE AND WATCH YOU
COME & GO
WHILE I'M IN A DIFFERENT CAR & DIFFERENT LOOK
EVERYDAY
I WILL POSE AS THE CABLE COMPANY & PLANT
CAMERAS & BUGS
AROUND THE HOUSE SO I CAN LISTEN TO YOU &
WATCH YOU
WATCH YOU TAKE A SHOWER LISTEN TO YOU TALK
ON THE PHONE
WATCH YOU COOK & EAT, LISTEN AND WATCH YOU
WHEN YOU HAVE COMPANY

YOU SEE ME EVERY DAY & YOU ARE CLUELESS TO WHO
I AM
DON'T KNOW IF I AM JOANN, MONIQUE, LISA, OR PAM
YOU AIN'T EVEN ALL THAT – I JUST HAVE NOTHING
ELSE TO DO
THAT'S WHY IMMA KEEP ON STALKING YOU
DON'T TRY TO GET A RESTRAINING ORDER, YOU
DON'T KNOW ME
PIECE OF PAPER DON'T MEAN NOTHING TO ME
IMMA KEEP ON MESSING WITH YOU; I AIN'T GON LET
YOU BE
IMMA GET INSIDE YOUR MIND. YOU GON LOOK OVER
YOUR SHOULDER FOR ME
WHEN I PASS BY YOU IN THE GROCERY STORE & SAY
"HI, HOW ARE YOU"
YOU WILL DOUBLE LOOK LIKE "I KNOW YOU FROM
SOMEWHERE…"

*AS I WALK AWAY I SMIRK – THINKING ABOUT WHERE
I WILL STALK YOU NEXT
ONE DAY YOU PARKED YOUR CAR IN THE DRIVEWAY
BUT I MOVED IT ON THE STREET*

*ANOTHER DAY YOU PULLED THE CAR INTO THE
DRIVEWAY
BUT WHEN YOU CAME OUT, IT WAS BACKED IN
THOUGHT YOU BOUGHT WHOLE MILK
BUT I REPLACED IT WITH SKIM MILK WHILE YOU WERE
AT WORK
YOU WALKED DOWN YOUR HALL IN THE HOUSE AND
DID A DOUBLE
LOOK AT A PICTURE ON THE WALL IT USED TO BE A
PICTURE OF YOU
AND YOUR GIRLFRIEND NOW, IT'S ONLY OF YOU
I ACCIDENTLY BUMPED INTO YOU AT STAR BUCKS
AND AGAIN YOU SAID YOU KNOW ME FROM
SOMEWHERE
AND FOR THANKSGIVING & CHRISTMAS AND THE
FAMILY REUNION
ALL THREE TIMES YOU ASK "WHOSE DAUGHTER ARE
YOU AGAIN?"*

*AS I WAS WATCHING YOU AT THE MALL WHILE YOU
DIDN'T NOTICE
CAUSE WHEN YOU LOOK, I TURN QUICKLY
YOU FINALLY CAME UP TO ME &INTRODUCED
YOURSELF
AND ASKED FOR MY NAME & NUMBER
NOW THAT WE'RE DATING I HAVE 1ST HAND ACCESS
TO BE OBSESSED WITH YOU
NOW I HAVE TO BE MORE CREATIVE WITH THE WAY I
STALK YOU
I'M NOT CRAZY – I JUST WANT TO BE OBSESSED WITH
YOU
SO I CAN STALK YOU & HARASS YOU
CAUSE THAT'S WHAT I DO*

I'M SICK & TIRED

I'm sick & tired of being cut off on the highway
I'm sick & tired of always having to be the nice one
I'm sick & tired of lending out my money & not getting paid
back
I'm sick & tired of men looking at my ass when walk away
I'm sick & tired of people choosing which part of the faith
They're going to practice
I'm sick & tired of cutting my grass every week
I'm sick & tired of listening to lies
I'm sick & tired of being broke, broke ass men, broke ass
Women, broke ass family
I'm sick & tired of being overworked & underpaid
I'm sick & tired of my phone ringing before 10 am
I'm sick & tired of bill collectors calling my house
I'm sick & tired of my check already being spent before I
even get paid
I'm sick & tired of botha's putting hickies on me cock
blocking
I'm sick & tired of botha's calling me sexy because my
interpretation is that they've already had me every
which way possible
I'm sick & tired of neighbors coming over to borrow a cup of
sugar
I'm sick & tired of studying
I'm sick & tired of cosigning
I'm sick & tired of paying a house note
I'm sick & tired of paying a car note
I'm sick & tired of having Menes cycles
I'm sick & tired of dusting
I'm sick & tired of working
I'm sick & tired of doing house work
I'm sick & tired of being sick & tired

I'M SPOILED

I thought I'd be better off by myself
But you made it impossible for me to love anybody else
I don't even know why I left you
'Cause he can't love me like you do boo
And until now, I never knew
I'm spoiled by your love - I'm spoiled by your touch
I didn't know this would hurt so much
Tryna get over you is a waste of time
The kinda love you give me is hard to find

I tried to tell myself that I'd be ova you
In a week or two, but to myself I lied
'Cause I have flashbacks of how you dip inside
Part my lips like the red sea as you penetrate deep within me
But you reached past the oz of my cervix – you touched my soul
That's how I know I'm spoiled by your love – I'm spoiled by your touch
Tryna get u otta my mind is a waste of time
'Cause your kinda love is so hard to cum across
C my love is the employee & your love is my boss

I tried another relationship a year ago
But in my heart, I just couldn't let go
My heart has been filled by you and there's just no more room
What am I tryna prove – shit, I'm helpless when it comes to you
I'm spoiled by ur love – I'm spoiled by your touch
I didn't know it would hurt this much
Tryna get ova you is a waste of time
The love you give me is so hard to find

Your touch, your touch, damn your touch
Caressing my body up & down I can't get enough
Sometimes I think you have 8 hands like an octopus
While my ass in the air, nose in my hole & mouth around my puss
Yes, I'm spoiled by your love – spoiled by your touch
Tryna get you otta my mind is a waste of time
Cuz ur kinda love is so hard to come across
Not having you is like having spaghetti & no sauce

Your touch is so deep
Just the thought of you – I begin to seep
When I'm lying in bed alone
More thoughts of you and I pump my hips & start to moan
I'm spoiled by ur love – I'm spoiled by your touch
I didn't know separation would hurt so much
Tryna get ova you is a waste of time
Cuz ur kinda love is so hard to find

65

I'M TENDER-HEADED

I thank God for Madam C. J. Walker & Suzy Wig
I've got a head full of "beyond kinky – nappy – thick before it even reached my follicular cells.
Does it mean I'm less than black because I need a relaxer to help a sister out?
Does it mean I have self hate because I'm not sporting locks?

Pressing comb was traumatizing as a child. I can still hear momma say, "That's the heat"
It makes my hair looks silky but that's a lot of pulling & such.
My hair goes from 1 inch to 10 inches….that's way too much pain.
Can't do twisties because locks pull my scalp
But with a perm I can just wash it & put it up in a wrap.

But when I feel like a kinky kinda look, I just wash my hair, braid it, let it dry then take the braids down. two strands or twist out

Madam C J Walker hooked me up. She gave me a variety of beauty selections.
If I want sista curls, I just set my hair on magnetic rollers & I'm looking fly.
Oh yeah, thank you Suzy Wig because if I want to be 2 inches all the way up to 19 inches,
Then back down to 6 inches, Suzy has my back!

Wrapped up, knots, Indian braids, French braids, plats,
Wet look, dry look, blonde to black and all colors in between.
Bald, French roll, kinky curly, wavey, Shirley temple, straw curls

So what you're natural! Natural or not it doesn't stop the pain!
What hair do I choose, it's my prerogative – I'm tender-headed.

IN THE BEGINNING GOD CREATED SEX

In the beginning God created the heavens and the earth
And on the 6th day God created man
But man woke up every day with an erection
And God said to the Holy Spirit and Jesus "wud u take a look at
that"
And the three continued to watch Adam

Adam began to explore himself. He took his finger & poked
at it a couple of times.
Then he felt some tingling & the sensation stunned him so
reflexively he grabbed it.
And within a matter of seconds Adam came hard and fast.

And God looked at the Holy Spirit and looked at Jesus and said
"Adam is happy but we can make him happier"
The Holy Spirit said "we need to complete him."
So God caused Adam to fall into a deep sleep
Then Jesus said "let us create beauty, perfection & sexy"
So God took a rib from Adam and formed woman.

And when Eve woke up with Adam
They were so happy to see each other they embraced
But his erection startled her and at the same time the softness of
her breast against his chest caused him to pre-cum.
Eve smelled his sweet juices
And wanted to taste. She got on her knees and licked it.
And when more pre-cum appeared, she licked it again

She found that the more she licked, the more he dripped
And his sensation continued to grow while his knees buckled
Instinctively she took him into her mouth and drank him
And he came better than the 1st time & Eve swallowed
And the 3 above saw that fallatio was good

And the 3 had a meeting while Adam & Eve slept
And the 2 said to God "com'mon O.G. there has got to be more"
A few hours later when Adam and Eve awakened in spoon
position,
Eve's ass was pressed against Adam, reflexively he put it in.
Eve said, "That's the wrong hole!" and Adam said
"It can't be wrong when it feels so right, just a little tight"
So eve took it (in doggy style) like a women who enjoyed pleasing
her husband.

Adam took his left hand and cuffed her right breast
With her nipple between his fingers
He took his right hand and put it between her legs
And when she'd squirt, he'd catch it
And they came – together; and as they laid post coital
Adam put the fingers from his right hand in his mouth
She tasted good so he flipped her and began to lick her

When his tongue spread her labia, he discovered her clitoris.
And when he flicked it with the tip of his tongue,
She began to flow with a sweet nectar so of course he drank her
The more he flicked her clit the more her sweet juices flowed
The more he flicked her clit, the more she made those sounds and
thrust her hips

Eve started to thrust all about like she was in an epileptic seizure
While she yelled "oh God, oh God, oh God".
The three above were still watching & God was pleased
With a smile on his face He said "they will always praise My
Name"
Mean while Adam came up for air and met her breast
He took her breast into his mouth and entered her for round two

JUST REST

NO MORE PAIN   NO MORE CRYING

NO MORE CRIME   NO MORE HATERS

NO MORE FEAR   NO MORE ANXIETY

NO MORE SICKNESS   NO MORE ACHES

NO MORE DISTRESS   NO MORE HATRED

NO MORE COMPLACENCY   NO MORE CROSS TO BARE

NO MORE "RELIGION"   NO MORE LONELINESS

NO MORE SMILING FACES, LYING TO THE RACES

NO MORE ROUGH SIDE OF THE MOUNTAIN

JUST PEACE   JUST LOVE   JUST REST

LAST NIGHT I HAD A DREAM

Last night I had a dream that u & I went for a boat ride
You helped me in, pushed off slowly, and then, you joined me in
the boat.
You rowed away from shore at a nice slow pace.
The sun was beaming- my smile was gleaming.
Soon enough there was no sight of shore.
The sun began to fade in and out of the clouds,
Until, the clouds took over.
The wind began to shift — our — boat.
Oh, there was a storm approaching
You held me tight, the only protection I had.
I squeezed you so tight and closed my eyes.
At the peak of the storm the boat started swaying
And rocking and tossing us all around
The winds were blowing, I was screaming,
As we were tossed and turned and we rocked here and there.
Our boat was moving faster & faster and faster until...
The winds ceased. The boat steadied.
Then before you knew it the sun began to creep back through
the clouds.
You relaxed your grip on me and — I — exhaled!
I just smirked in amazement — you rowed us back to shore
Just like you started, at a nice slow pace.

LAY OVER

I was on my way to California. But I had a 3 hour layover in
Utah.
While I was waiting at grate 16, I started to nod off to sleep.
I was so sleepy but I couldn't help but to notice this
gorgeous man.
He was waiting near grate 14, noticing me looking peaceful.

My blinks became longer & longer & seemed like with
Each blink he became closer & closer.
I smelled an erotic scent that caused me to smile in my sleep.
I awakened to find myself caressed against his chest.

With his arms wrapped around me while stroking my hair.
I looked into his eyes and our lips met.
Just then, his flight was announced to board to Washington.
I watched him walk away & disappear into the plane.

Let's Take a Trip to the Bathroom

Laying in bed just kinda looking at the ceiling
Thinking about what it would feel like to tickle my clitoris
So I reach down below & dang, she's already hot & wet

But she sure could stand to be a little wetter

So I head to the bathroom & I run some water
I put my hand under the running water to make sure it's about 98.7
degrees
About the same as a man's mouth

I slip otta my silk – tip toe first into the tub
While the water's running, I lay on my back & spread eagle on the
wall
So the running water can run right on top of my split

My insides pulsate and I start fiending for more
I stand up & take hold of the shower head
I look down & spread my lips & aim the shower head
Right in the middle & each time the water strikes

Against my clitoris, my knees buckle & I get light headed
As the water runs down my leg, I can't tell if its
Water or my cum – then the next morning

I wake up in the tub smiling & remember what
Put me to sleep
Oops, I did it again

LORD HELP ME

Lord help me 'cause I just heard his voice on the phone
Lord help me 'cause he's on his way over & im home alone
Lord help me 'cause with this man I don't know how to be strong
Lord help me 'cause day by day I struggle between right & wrong

Lord help me since I'm home alone there will be no cock blocking
Lord help me 'cause tonight there may be two bodies rocking
Lord help me 'cause my hormones on the inside are hopping
Lord help me 'cause I'm not try to let it be on & popping

Lord help me 'cause after my hugs, he has mad erections
Lord help me 'cause I'm trying my best not to think of my multi-
*   ejections*
Lord help me 'cause his touch gives me pilo-erections
Lord help me 'cause I feel the wetness from his pre-ejections

Lord help me I don't wanna seem selfish 'cause You bless me with wet
*   dreams*
But Lord help me 'cause I just imagine what I would do with my tongue
*   ring*
Lord help me 'cause I can't help but to imagine sexual things
Lord help me 'cause I fiend for that post coital gleam

Lord help me 'cause I can't get him off my mind
Lord help me 'cause he's so d@mn fine
Lord help me 'cause I'm having withdrawals 'cause it's been months/years
*   pass time*
Lord help me 'cause I really don't mean to whine

Lord help me 'cause it's too much going on in my brain
Lord help me 'cause this man's touch drives me insane
Lord help me 'cause I can't stand the rain
Lord help me 'cause a better Christian is what I'm tryna obtain

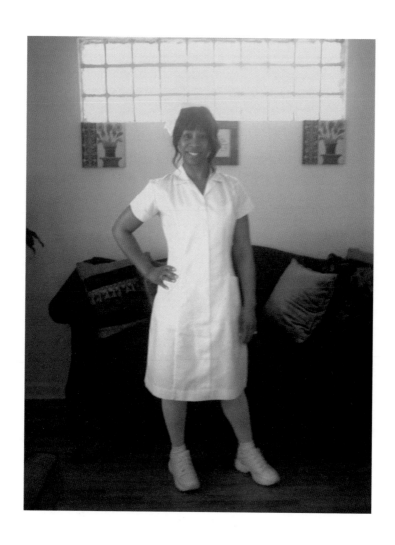

LOVE AT FIRST SIGHT

*She has my smile, my lips, my nose. She weighed 6lbs
13oz. She has a passion for education & career; desire
for love. She's adventurous – not afraid to conquer the
world. She has empathy for others. Her heart weighs
heavy when she craves answers. She loves to read,
disciplined; she's strong for her sibling. Graduated
magna cud laude'. She's strong minded & willed; very
direct. Speaks like a natural born interrogator. Has no
problem sharing. She is: inquisitive & energetic,
adventurer, broadminded, extroverted, optimistic,
enthusiastic about life, can be impossible to keep
down, love change & adapts to change, great sense of
humor, generous, wear clothes for comfort not style
unless necessary, tomboy like*

*She has my smile, my eyes, my walk. She weighed 7
lbs. She is free-spirited. She comes and goes as the
wind blows. She won't settle. She is not your average.
She is still discovering and adventuring. She has a
strong sensual side. She has natural hand tremors. She
has a sweet exterior but gangster interior. She is
strong, she is a survivor. She is: understanding, gentle,
affectionate. She's easy going & generally accepting to
others around her with different personalities. She
gives of herself emotionally. She's strong and vibrant
to any cause she put her heart to. She's intuitive,
compassionate to animals. Her face shows emotions.*

He has my smile & my nose. He weighed 8 lbs. he is happy go lucky and everybody's friend. he loves helping and a natural at nurturing others. He has a strong zeal for his siblings, cousins, & family. He is humorous, tall, smart, handsome, and carefree. He is: deeply intuitive, sentimental, emotions run strong, sympathetic, attuned to those around him, devoted, wonderful to be around, compassionate, fierce protection of the one he loves, and tenacity/persistent.

He has my eyes & my smile. He loves knives & swords like me. He weighed 6 lbs. he has beautiful chocolate skin. He made the biggest transformation over the years. He studies people. He's mostly introverted with extroverted moments. He loves cars and money. He is: professional bound, keeps values & traditions close, tackles life in conventional ways, serious minded, independent, leads to progress in personality, job responsible, good mannered, disciplined, self controlled, dark sense of humor.

God blessed me with beautiful children who were all made in love, loved before I even laid eyes on them, born surrounded by love, raised with an angel's touch of love, wooven to share love. They are God's gift to me.

LOVE GREATER THAN ETERNITY

*THERE WAS AN ANGEL WHO FELL IN LOVE WITH A
HUMAN.
HE ASKED GOD TO ALLOW HIM TO BECOME HUMAN SO
HE COULD BE WITH HER.
GOD TOLD HIM IF HE ALLOWED THIS, THERE IS NO
TURNING BACK.
ONE DAY THE WOMAN WAS RIDING BY ON HER BIKE &
FOUND HIM LYING IN THE PARK.
SHE AWAKENED HIM TO SEE IF HE WAS ALRIGHT.
HE SAID YES, HE MUST HAVE FALLEN ASLEEP.
THEY REALIZED THEY HAD CHEMISTRY & EXCHANGED
NUMBERS.
THEY TALKED EVERYDAY SOMETIMES FALLING ASLEEP
ON THE PHONE.
THEY WERE GOING TO GO ON A DATE AT THE END OF THE
WEEK.
HE SAT AT A DINER WAITING FOR HER AND SOON SAW
HER RIDING HER BIKE TOWARD HIM.
HE SMILED.
THEN HE ALSO SAW A TRUCK APPROACHING OUT OF
CONTROL,
BUT SHE COULDN'T SEE BECAUSE SHE WAS BUSY
WAVING & SMILING AT HIM.
WHEN THE TRUCK HIT HER, SHE DIED INSTANTLY.
AT FIRST HE WAS MAD AT GOD.
BUT, THEN REALIZED THE ONE DAY HE MET HER & THE
FEW NIGHTS HE GOT TO TALK TO HER ON THE PHONE...
WAS WORTH MORE THAN AN ETERNITY IN HEAVEN.*

MAKING LOVE WITH UNSPOKEN WORDS

I had a few things on my mind, but I'd rather not say
So let me make love to you in a different way

Now for my bag of goodies:

CONDOMS: Ribbed condoms, edible condoms, magnum condoms
We will always know our status-------------------->MESSAGE!

BLIND FOLD – will enhance the other sense
---> listen – as I whisper sweet nothings in your ear
---> smell – strawberries and champaign from Victoria's Secret
---> touch - as you only can imagine where your hands will explore
        Yes, touch can have you fiending for so much more

EDIBLE BODY LOTION/SPRAY
---> taste - & guess which body part &/or chocolates you like best
        We're just getting started – its no time to rest

TICKLE WHIP – feel the softness just like roses petals
        And anticipate what will be spanked next

HAND CUFFS – no choice in the matter to be
        Vulnerable, and in suspense, and totally submissive
        Be a good boy cause I'm on a mission

Now that foreplay, is out of the way
Let's get to the prize, just sit back and let me ride
If you like it from the front, you will have multiple choices
---> left breast ---> right breast ---> neck ---> ears
If you'd like for me to turn around
Feel free to put your lip on my back or my right or left cheek
Or my Georgia peach or where ever they can reach
Of course there's another way for you to be pleased
I can always get on my knees

MASSA'S LOVE

octane, orangutan, half-breed, jig-a-boo, house nigga, porch
monkey, tar-baby, spook, spick, colored, niggra, trash

"momma, you love daddy?" momma said "yeah baba"
"then why ya'll always mad when u get back from massa's house?"
Momma didn't say a word, just kept on braiding my hair

One day we's pickn cotton, singing songs to glory
Sun beaming, I'm thirsty, sweaty, hot & tired
Ol massa said, "why don't you come get some cold water from the
big house"

Momma said, "please massa she ain't thirsty – she be alryte!"
Massa raised his whip. Momma closed her eyes & fell on her knees
& continued to beg "she only 13, please!"
Daddy act like he ain't see or hear nothing – just kept on pickin
cotton

When we got to the big house massa told all the house niggas to
go to the store
While his wife was already in town shopping for a new dress for
their anniversary

Massa poured me a tall glass of cold water himself
With a wicked grin on his face. I said, "thank ya massa.
I better git back to those fields & pick that cotton."
Massa grabbed me by the arm, said, "now girl how u gon pay for
dat water?"

I said, "massa, u no we's ain't got no money – cain't pay you n food 'cause all our food comes from you."

Massa said, "com'mere girl, you gon pay in a way yo momma & my wife cain't"

Out in the fields no body was working. Only cries 'cause all they heard were my screams

Massa made me walk back to the fields & git back to work

As I walked off the porch, massa's wife & the house niggas sitting in the wagon

The house niggas dropped their headed while massa's wife glared at me like I did something wrong.

Erbody pickn cotton like they don't know nothing bout what happened

Don't care how I hurt. I started pickn cotton again

while blood trickled down my legs, pooled around my ankle & stained between my toes

now I know why momma & daddy always mad when she get back from massa's house

and I know why we so many names & colors like octane, orangutan, half-breed, jig-a-boo, house nigga, porch monkey, tar-baby, spook, spick, colored, niggra, trash

MISS HAPPY JUICE

I'm happy cause the sky is blue, happy cause the sky is grey
I'm happy cause it's sunny outside, happy cause it's about to rain
I'm happy cause I have a job, happy cause I love my job
I'm happy cause I have children, happy cause they're off to school
I'm happy cause I can walk, happy I have a choice to talk
I'm happy cause it's year two thousands = happy cause I'm not picking
      cotton
I'm happy cause I have a bathroom, happy cause there's no outhouse
I'm happy cause I have a car, happy cause I wrote a poem
I'm happy cause someone smiled at me, happy jus looking at new born
      babies
I'm happy cause I gotta fresh perm, happy I ate a big mac
I'm happy cause my Mohawk rocks & happy about my afro puffs
I'm happy I've got education, happy I'm in my right mind
I'm happy for my reasonable portion of my health & strength
I'm happy Jesus saved my soul
I'm so happy I could play hop scotch from Mercury & Venus, to Mars &
Jupiter, to Saturn, Uranus, to Neptune & Pluto, back to earth again

MR A.M.

He is more like a morning person; I call him "Mr AM"
I am more like a night person; he calls me "Ms PM"
But somehow we've got to meet in the middle
I wish I could reach him but he won't allow me
But I can see in his eyes, he likes what he sees
When he stared into my eyes, he put voodoo on me
Now I have to see him & be with him
What I want, is a hug what I need, is his hug
I just want him to hold me; well I daydream about him holding me
But I'm afraid of his touch; it just may be a lil too much
But also in my daydreams I kiss his cheek, then he smiles
And he looks at me and makes me smile — he calls me beautiful with his eyes, with his smile
But he's so distant, he knows but he doesn't know
He wants me but he doesn't want me
Sooner or later he will figure it out
That either he can love a woman like me or he will keep spoiling himself
This is weird but not really weird,
I was his sheep, but I graduated to his jewel
Winds be blowing him my way but he goes against it; he goes his way
Hopeless restless, he'll be back because he can't go against the winds
It just slows him, but eventually he delayed the inevitable
Or he let his blessing slip through his fingers
And he knows this

MR LEWIS BAKER

*IN THE MIDDLE OF THE NIGHT, SOMEONE CREPT INTO MY
BED
I WAS IN A DEEP SLEEP SO I THOUGHT I WAS DREAMING;
SOMEONE GOT IN MY BED
I FELT PRESSURE ON MY BODY BUT NO ONE WAS THERE
I FELT LIPS SUCKING AND HANDS STROKING THROUGH MY
HAIR
I WAS SO TIRED, I WENT BACK TO SLEEP
BUT FOR SOME REASON I HAD ADDED BODY HEAT
FELT DEEP PENETRATION ALTHOUGH THERE WAS NO
MASTURBATION
I AWAKENED THE NEXT MORNING WITH SUCH A GLEAM
BECAUSE I THOUGHT I HAD YET, ANOTHER WET DREAM*

*15YRS AGO MR BAKER DIED IN MY HOUSE
RECENTLY HIS SOUL WAS AWAKENED AND HIS SPIRIT WAS
AROUSED
LAST MONTH MY NIECE WATCHED HIM AS HE LOOKED OUT
THE BACK WINDOW
TWO WEEKS AGO MY DAUGHTER WAS SITTING IN THE
LIVING ROOM
AS HE WALKED DOWN THE HALL TO THE FRONT DOOR, LIKE
HE WAS ABOUT TO GO
I WONDER WHILE I'M TAKING A SHOWER IF HE'S WATCHING
ME
WONDER DOES HE ENJOY WHAT HE SEES
SOMEBODY'S ENERGY HAS BROUGHT HIM BACK & I NEED TO
KNOW
'CAUSE MR BAKER IS GONNA HAVE TO GO*

MY PRAYER IS TO HEAL THE LAND

II Chronicles 7:14 If my people which are called by my name, shall humble themselves, and pray, and seek my face, and turn from their wicked ways; then will I hear from heaven, and will forgive their sins , and will heal their land.

Innocent blood in the land, so much killing in the land; people are dying, children & grown folk crying – in the land

My prayer is to heal the land

Drive-by shootings in the land, we need to take a stand, where do our children play, sometimes it's too hard to pray; do I even want to stay – in this land

My prayer is to heal the land

HIV, HPV, HSV spreading through the land; if we could reach one teach one starting with one man. There is hatred in the land, so much crime in the land; no love in the land

My prayer is to heal the land

So much trouble in the land, muggers & robbers, dope and drugs in the land; they say one shot in the vein you'll feel no pain. But that stain will remain FOREVER!

My prayer is to heal the land

haters, vanity, lost souls, depression, suicidal thoughts, child molesters, homeless people, jobless people, in the land. rich getting richer, poor getting poorer, foreclosures on homes, contaminated food in the land

my prayer is to heal the land

There's prejudice in the land, no justice in the land, no rest no peace, no love in the land. Abuse in the land, alcohol use in the land. Drunk driving, lives lost, nobody sees nothing but who pays the cost.

My prayer is to heal the land.

Eph 5:5 whoremonger, unclean person, covetous men, adulterers in the land

My prayer is to heal the land.

Rom 1:30 backbiters, haters of God, despiteful, proud, boasters, inventors of evil things disobedient to parents – in the land.

My prayer is to heal the land

Rev 21:8 & 22:15 fearful, unbelieving, abominable, murders, sorcerers, idolaters, liars.

My prayer is to heal the land

Mark 7:22 Thefts, covetousness, wickedness, deceit, lasciviousness, an evil eye, blasphemy, pride, foolishness

My prayer is to heal the land

Galations 5:19 other works of the flesh are manifest, which are these; Adultery, fornication, uncleanness, lasciviousness

My prayer is to heal the land

If God's people which are called by His name, if we would just humble ourselves
And seek His face while we're down on our knees praying
And if we let go of the wicked things we hold on to
Then will God hear from heaven, and he will forgive our sin sick souls
It's that simple – then God will heal our land

NEW BEGINNINGS

Why do you keep asking, "why me?"
It's not something you can plainly see

I'm sure God will bring things to light
Make things as clear as day & night

But for now we will enjoy this moment
Too excited to be content

I love the way my stomach get these butterflies
Sometimes you throw me off & make me tongue tied

My souls seems to fall deep in your smile
You especially have a charismatic style

When you wrap your arms around me
I close my eyes & say, 'what could this be?'

You bring out something from deep within
Thoughts of you – send chill bumps to my skin

The sound of your voice is like music to my ears
I'm anxious to see what may come in years

Even if nothing develops, we should remain great friends
Hope you're a part of my life 'til the end

Newly Found Love

Do I have to let go of a newly found potential love?
Feels like a spoonful of heaven from above
This big fine hunk of a man
Make me weak in the knees, I can hardly stand
I'd miss your smile your style your intelligence
I'd miss laying close to you, head buried in your chest
Oh how I feel your hands over my body like it's a work
    Of art
But the end may be near & we'll have to part
Maybe I was meant to bring into your life a little
    sunshine
And put a lil som'em som'em on your mind
Maybe I was sent an angel to show me a thing or two
I sometimes feel like as if I don't really know what to
    do
But you'll show me and guide me and teach me what I
    Should know
And when I try to run, you'll block me & there'll be no
    Where to go
I'll run right into your arms
Smitten by your hidden charms
I think we will eventually grow
There are lots of things we must get to know
We'll start by being friends
We'll go from there & maybe it'll never have to end

NO WEAPON

No weapon shall be formed against me
No weapon against my children, my job, my marriage,
Not against my relationship with my Lord & Savior

No weapon formed in my kids shall come against me:
breaking curfew, wanting to talk back, being hard
headed & disobedient, thinking grown ups are stupid,
playing hooky from school, stealing, cursing

No weapon formed at my job shall come against me:
skipped over for promotion, firing, demotions,
downsizing, different attitudes & spirits, provoking
spirits,

No weapon formed in my marriage shall come against
me: cheating, arguing, not happy, lack of
communication, together but separate, lack of
forgiveness, woman wanting to be the head, man abusing
his authority, lack of intimacy in bed, evil stares, cursing
& fussing

No weapon shall come against me with my relationship
with God: not my own recklessness, slowfullness,
selfishness, bitterness, disobedience, orneriness, anger,
infidelities, quenching of His spirit

**NO WEAPON FORMED AGAINST ME SHALL
PROSPER**

ORDER MY STEPS

Order my steps in Your word dear Father
Why do I request this - when obedience I probably
won't bother
How can You lead me guide me everyday...
When I think I'm grown, I know everything; I can find
my own way?
You see, You tell me to go right, I choose to go left;
I ask Your help, but it waste my breath.
Narrow is the way that so few choose,
Broad is the way we often go but we always lose.

If You order my steps, I will be set up with riches in
glory & mansions...
End up in heaven with my Father, my big Brother, my
family, singing & dancing.
But instead of going to Bible study or just pick up my
Bible & study it,
I choose to hang out with my friends, out partying &
clubbin it.
You order me to go to church on Sunday, but I choose
to wash my car...
I may creep off with an insignificant other to a hotel
somewhere far...
I may even decide to get drunk at my local pub and
bar.
You order me to visit the sick and the elderly of the
church
But instead, I've got to watch my soaps, get my hair
done, or go shopping for a new purse.

You order me to give my offering and give my tithes;
OOPS! I better watch out before I get some evil eyes.
You order me to hold my peace when I wanna cut
somebody,
Turn the other cheek like Jesus – not act like a
heathen so rowdy.

Often times we wanna put the blame on the devil, but, we give him way too much credit.

We need to take a look in the mirror & point at ourselves & stop being so pathetic!
I want God to anoint me, but He can't bless me
Cause I'm not worthy, cause I corrupt me!

God, You've been teaching me Your will from day one.
I've got the nerves to be stubborn not to get on my knees & humble myself before Your son?
I don't even have the patience while waiting on Your will
So I try to speed things along& make it my will.
You keep trying to work on me by molding me and making me
But I'm so hard-headed, I keep reshaping me.
Dangit – there I go again, I keep messin and messin
I'm messing up my blessings.

Take charge of my thoughts so I can speak right, think right, be right, walk right
But I know imma have to meditate, affirmate, no abbreviate, 24/7 relate to Your Word day & night.
Bridle my tongue so what's pleasing to You, I can say....
Expelling happy, positive words of encouragement day by day.
When my daily conversation has words of profane,
Or I get ready to curse someone out, I should be ashamed,
Jus going off...looking like a fool disgracing Your blessed and Holy name.
Order my tongue so when I speak, I speak words that are Godly
Not words that are foul, rude, or worldly.

That's why when we sing that song we get so emotional
Cuz we cause our own life to be so roller coasternal.
We beg of You to order our steps, order our words, order or tongue,
Guide our feet, wash our heart, keep us from doing wrong.

Show us how to walk, show us how to talk
Basic instructions before leaving the earth is what we should stalk.
People come people go, trends come & go, the world is always in a change,
You say "I AM" because You're here yesterday, today, & forever – You are still the same
Submissively we ask You to order our steps so we can faithfully praise Ur Name.

94

OUR FATHER

DAY ~ YESTERDAY IS GONE, IT'S NO MORE ~
TOMORROW IS NOT PROMISED

OUR DAILY OUR FATHER ~ YOUR FATHER ~ MY FATHER

WHICH ART IN HEAVE ~ NOT OF THIS WORLD ~ THE
PROMISE LAND

HALLOWED BE THY NAME ~ JEHOVAH, JIRAH, MESSIAH ~
MASTER, TEACHER, SAVIOR

THY KINDOM COME ~ JESUS IS COMING BACK ~ KNOW
ONE KNOWS THE HOUR

THY WILL BE DONE ~ IT'S IN HIS WORD BELIEVE IT ~
THAT'S THAT

IN EARTH AS IT IS IN HEAVEN ~ WE WILL INHERIT THE
EARTH ~ WE WILL REIGN WITH HIM

GIVE US THIS BREAD ~ BASIC INSTRUCTIONS BEFORE
LEAVING THE EARTH ~ STUDY TO SHOW MYSELF
APPROVED

FORGIVE US OUR DEBTS ~ YOU ARE SINNERS SAVED BY
GRACE ~ I AM NOT PERFECT

AS WE FORGIVE OUR DEBTORS ~ FORGIVE 7 X 70 ~
TEACH ME UNCONDITIONAL LOVE

LEAD US NOT INTO TEMPTATION ~ PUT ON THE WHOLE
ARMOR ~ GIVE ME A SPIRITUAL EYE

BUT DELIVER US FROM EVIL ~ YIELD NOT UNTO
TEMPTATION ~ I WILL STAND STRONG

FOR THINE IS THE KINGDOM ~ THE NEW JERUSALEM ~
THE STREETS ARE MADE OF GOLD

AND THE POWER ~ GOD HAS ALL POWER ~ WONDER
WORKING POWER

AND THE GLORY ~ GOD GETS THE GLORY ~ GLORY TO
GOD IN THE HIGHEST

PAIN ~ PLEASURE ~BITTERSWEET

PAIN IS

Being married & together with my children's father for 16 years

Til he broke my heart & I cried so much I thought I had no more tears

PAIN IS

Pulling a 9mm on him & pulling the trigger twice

Cause I wanted him to feel my pain & hurt, but I didn't aim to take his life

PAIN IS

Going into a depression were I couldn't even give myself a bath

My friends and family tried to help make me smile – I couldn't even laugh

PAIN IS

My four hearts went thru suicidal thoughts & separation anxiety but I counseled them with love

But what held us together was my family support & God's love from above

PAIN IS

Being raised by a mom who never initiated an 'I love you' or a hug first

Couldn't understand why I felt lonely or why my feelings were easily hurt

PAIN IS

Being celibate for three years waiting on my Mr. Right to find me

When he did, he was just wrong spelled like R. O. N. G.

PAIN IS

Watching my close friend endure physical abuse I confused it with a 12 round bout

While we were planning and scheming for her way out

PAIN IS

Seeing my niece & nephew emotional because their dad refused to be a constant in the house

Cause every time things are perfect & correct, he wants to find trouble & bounce

PAIN IS

Having a job where death, sickness, and pain in one form or another is all around me

Spiritual, physical, & emotional is how I see it

PAIN IS

Having one of my sons put into the system because of lies some hot heifer told

Felt like my baby was ripped from my wound without cutting the umbilical cord & he's only 15yrs old

PAIN IS

Even though that heifer recanted her story the next day

They detained my baby five more days

PAIN IS

Just when I thought I cried all my tears

I cried over my baby; I could've filled the next ten thousand years

PLEASURE IS

That same baby daddy who thought the grass was greener & caused so much hurt

Got over there & found out that is blue & covered with dirt

PLEASURE IS

That in my rage the clip wasn't in the 9mm all the way but I was maaad as a mother

But thank God my children were spared their father & mother

PLEASURE IS

Outsiders couldn't tell we were divorced because we functioned well, cuz our children were priority

our children are so happy & they stopped having separation anxiety

PLEASURE IS

That same daughter with suicidal thoughts & counseled by my love, received an award and was in the paper for scholar athlete, ranked #1 in her senior class, will finish her college major a year early as she becomes a FBI profiler. And she's just about to lounge her new business

PLEASURE IS

That same mom who didn't express her love the way I thought she should always cooked dinner, was at most all my track meets, volleyball games, and basketball games and

even though she still thinks I'm weird, she's my biggest
cheer leader

PLEASURE IS

Now that my Mr. Rong is gone, I can walk into my house
and smell peace and that's priceless

PLEASURE IS

Watching my friend get out of that abusive relationship
Only to receive love that she's never felt before

PLEASURE IS

Seeing my niece & nephew resilient & honor
My sister as mother and father

PLEASURE IS

I love my job and for me it's a blessing
Nurturing and loving is my calling

PLEASURE IS

That same 15 year old who was robbed of five days of his
life, has been to the junior Olympic in track & field 4 times,
and three times to the national youth football
championship with MD boys & girls club. In high school
playing football: offense = tight end & wide receiver,
Defense = corner back & safety

PLEASURE IS

That 15 year old can talk to me about the 100th number of
Psalm and tell me "everything's' going to be alright".
And as for that ignorant detective who wanted to make my
son guilty VENGENCE IS MINE SAYETH THE LORD & a lil help
from me and my lawyer

BITTER SWEET

Life's growing pains does not out weight my growing
pleasures

PRESS ON

Mark 5:27- 29
When she heard of Jesus, came in the press behind and touched his
garment. For she said, if I may touch but His clothes, I shall be
whole. And straightway the fountain of her blood was dried up;
and she felt in her body that she was healed of that plague.

I'm walking this daily walk & it aint easy
I must press on

Satan tries to tear me down,
gray clouds come around
but I must press on

I feel so alone
I must press on

I feel when im slipping into a depression
But just one touch will start my progression
I must press on

Sometimes I can't find my way
Tomorrow will be a better day
I must press on

I keep on praying and calling
Cuz I stumble & keep on falling
I must press on

My burdens get me down
I keep getting turned around
I must press on

I look to the hills which cometh my help
I must press on

Though trials come on every hand
I must press on

Trouble don't last always
I must press on

I feel so hard headed sometimes
But He didn't give up on me

I must press on

Sometimes I fall
But He will pick me up & dust me off
I must press on

When I messed up He restores my soul
I must press on

When the storms of life are raging
I must press on

Sometimes it's hard to tell night from day
I must press on

There's no way I can live without you
I must press on

I would be nothing without you
I must press on

I need my joy restored
I must press on

I need a healing
I must press on

I need a miracle
I must press on

I need peace
I must press on

LIKE THE WOMAN WITH THE ISSUE OF BLOOD, KEEP PRESSING
ON. SHE KEPT PRESSING ON EVEN IN THE MULTITUDE OF
PEOPLE; JUST TO TOUCH THE HEM OF HIS GARMENT. PRESS ON
EVEN WHEN YOU CAN'T SEE THE LIGHT AT THE END OF THE
TUNNEL. KEEP PRESSING ON THROUGH ALL THE TRIALS,
TRIBULATIONS, & WIERINESS. YOUR FAITH WILL MAKE YOU
WHOLE OF YOUR PLAGUE. BUT REMEMBER, JESUS' WILL BE
DONE.

Pretend I'm Her

We sat at the hotel bar drowning in our own self-pity
Our eyes connected & we could see pain in each others' soul
We talked & revealed a sadness that weighed us down

His wife has been fighting cancer for 20yrs
Now she has metastasis to the brain
He takes care of her even though she no longer knows who he is,
He feels insane

I lost my virginity to a gang initiation – a gang rape
I have never felt loves' touch

I invited him up to my room just so I cud hold him - & he obliged
Once in the room, we sat on the edge of the bed in silence for an hour
He finally said he'd never been unfaithful to his wife
But he hasn't been intimate with her in over ten years
Now, she'll be dead soon & will leave him all alone
I told him – he could replenish my faith in men if he'd just pretend I
was her

Then nothing was said again for a while only sounds made from
Touching & rubbing & sucking & licking & moaning & my insides
squishing
I didn't know a stroke could be so gentle & caring
The way he locked his fingers through my hair & kissed my neck
Was mesmerizing & succulent; I experienced my 1st climax
After he came we laid in each other's arms
I cud feel his tears running down onto my face

Then he said softly "I love you – we were supposed to have the rest of
life together"
"please don't leave me; we can beat this cancer."

After he cried himself to sleep – I slipped away in the middle of the
night
As I leaned on the door outside of the room,
I took a sigh of relief – feeling like a weight lifted off me

PRINCE PRINCESSES KINGS QUEENS RULERS & LEADERS

I know we have kings & queens in here
When we were born our parents didn't look at us and say
"he/she will grow to be a: prostitute, he/she will grow up to be lazy,
liars, backstabbers, robbers, ugly, drug dealers, moochers, deceivers"

And yes, we do have those in this world, you know them
They blame everyone but themselves
They blame willie lynch, "the man", their absentee father
The neighborhoods they grew up in, the families or situations they
were born into
They blame everyone but the man in the mirror

So, no, when our parents looked at us, they said
"he is beautiful, she is beautiful, you are beautiful"
Women, we are here to be companions & helpmeet for men, and
nurturers to our families
Men are here to protect us, provide for us, and preserve us.
When we stay together as a family, a unit, we can be a much stronger
nation
Because we should be our brothers' keeper, and it does take a village
to raise a child

But we have become so comfortable in our single parent homes;
leaving our women to take on dual identities or two parent homes
with a hostile environment,
Leaving our children to grow into a new norm of "this is how it was
this is how it's supposed to be"
But this is unacceptable when we see other nations come into our
home country
Building business', supporting one another, sticking together and
having each other's back
Instead we want to tear one another down, cut each other's throat

When our little girls see their dads hugging their moms
They feel that electricity of love and a seed is implanted
In their subconscious for their idea future husband
When mothers tell their sons to take out the trash

He instantly forms a tapestry that's embedded in his subconscious
This becomes one of the basics of responsibility for taking care
bigger things in life

When mothers and fathers look their little girls in the eyes to let
them know they are beautiful
And offer encouraging words, our little girls are not quick to seek
outside validation leading to unwanted and unwedded
pregnancies

When our children see us, their parents inviting company over
Holding hands in prayer & encouraging one another & having a
good time in harmony
They will grow to choose their friends wisely & grow to be role
models to their peers
When they see us knowing how to talk to one another with mutual
respect and common courtesy

And when they see that we are living the Christ-like lifestyle that
we profess with our mouth on Sunday
And being about our Father's business, then, boy girl man woman
can hold our heads up high
Then we can be our own heroes & sheroes
Then we can make goals and dreams that supersede what's
expected by "the others"

Although God said "Ask and it should be given"
We need to press on toward the mark which our forefathers
started
We need not to be complacent
We need not be discouraged or spoiled by the system that tries to
steer us
We need not think everything is to be spoon fed to us

In you, I see Malcolm x, Martin Luther, Mahalia & Aretha, Madam
CJ, Michelle & Barak, Miles Davis, Marvin Sapp, Lil Blind Boys of
Alabama, Maya Angelo, Sarah Boone – inventor of the ironing
board, Benjamin Bradley – steam engine, Patrica Bath –creator of
laser based cataract surgery, Charles Brooks –street sweeper,
George Washington Carver-numerous inventions, Matthew Cherry
–fenders on cars, George Crum – potato chips, Charles Drew –
blood preservation & the blood bank, Joseph Hawkins – metal
oven racks, Thomas Jennings – dry cleaning, Sarah Good –

folding bed, George Grant – improved the golf tee, James West – electric microphone, Garrett Morgan – hair straightening iron~gas mask~traffic signal. Daniel Hale Williams – 1st open heart surgeon, Ben Carson – first black brain surgeon, Ralph Gilles young black man designed the crysler 300 in 2005. Tony Hansberry II, a 14yr old black boy– 2009 invented a laparoscopic instrument to assist suturing in surgery. This list is endless and goes on & on.

Do you even know who you are?
We are business owners, evangelist, preachers, doctors, lawyers, FBI agents, engineers, surgeons,
We are Nurses, pharmacist, anesthesiologist, entrepreneurs, teachers, professors, musicians,
We are Songstress, police officers, firefighters, highway patrolmen, practitioners, photographers,
We are Executives, disaster response teams, secretaries, electricians, architects, plumbers, construction workers, ophthalmologists, interior designers, fashion designers, television broadcasters, book writers, inventors, mail carriers...the possibilities are endless

Do you even know who you are?
We are Christ's disciples
We are Gods' people
We are Gods' chosen ones
We are heir to the kingdom
We are more than conquerors

Step into your greatness
Step into your greatness
Step into your greatness
Step into your power!

YES! I see our young people as prince & princesses, who will grow to become kings & queens because they are our future leaders & rulers

PURGE

Purge hyssop & gossip from in and out of church
Purge yourself from depression
Purge yourself from alcoholism & drunkenness
Purge yourself from pornography in magazines & triple x movies
Purge yourself from doing just enough (Sunday morning Christians)
Purge yourself from abusing your wife and children
Purge yourself from molestation
Purge yourself from drugs, including cigarettes
Purge yourself from asphyxiation & strangulation
Purge yourself from suicidal thoughts
Purge yourself from being a hater
Purge yourself from negativity
Purge yourself from raping our queens
Purge yourself from telling part of the truth
Purge yourself from having ugly thoughts about your neighbor
Purge yourself from being disobedient to your parents
Purge yourself from obscene things in front of your children
Purge yourself from selling drugs poisoning our people
Purge yourself being lustful greedy needy dependant
Purge yourself wasting food when people in the world are starving
Purge yourself from being slowful, lazy, putting God's work last
Purge yourself selfish & unappreciative
Purge yourself from fornication, adultery, lesbianism, and homosexuality
Purge yourself lying, cheating, killing, (even murder in your thoughts)

PUT YOUR LIPS ON ME

Com'mon baby put your lips on me
What would happen, just wait & see
                Tie my hands up to the ceiling
                Make me have an erotic feeling
Lock your fingers thru my hair
Look into my eyes if you dare
                Bite my neck, just a little peck
                Kiss my spine – one at a time
Kiss my shoulders, biceps, triceps, & on down my arms
Supinate my hands & kiss my palms
                Now, hold my hips & kiss my back
                Then go all the way down – lick my crack
Kiss my ass – but not to fast
Baby make it last

                Spin me, flip me, make me wet
                Let's just see how far you'll get
Now take your tongue & tickle my nipple
Put your tongue tip on my clit
                Wrap your lips around my lips
                Make me moan & hit that high pitch
Kiss my knees – keep up the tease
Make me beg "baby please"
                Kiss my shin, Achilles, and top of my feet
                Baby when u untie me – im gon knock you off your feet
You've just kissed me from the top of my head – hair follicles
Let's not forget to suck those toes.

111

QUEEN OF HEARTS

Hearts don't fake, hearts ache, heart breaks
Heart fibulate, hearts don't lie, hearts beat
Hearts skips a beat, hearts pound,
hearts cheat, hearts speak, hearts cry,
heart palpitations, heart flutter,
heart arrythmia's, cold hearted, heart
stops, flat line_____

REBUILD ME FROM THIS BROKENESS

Rebuild me from the brokenness that separates me from You
Rebuild me from all the harm that I may do – to my soul
Rebuild me from this world that often finds its home on my shoulder
Rebuild me 'cause sometimes I feel like I've been ran over by a bulldozer
Rebuild me from the bitterness I hold & ill feelings from my broken home
Rebuild me 'cause sometimes it hurts so bad it feels like I've got broken bones
Rebuild me from this hurt, from disappointments, from all the pain
Rebuild these stains that remains embedded in my brain
Rebuild me from restless sleep, tossing & turning at nights
Rebuild me from past angers that causes me today to argue, fuss, & fight
Rebuild me from my broken kids, broken dreams, and all my fears
Rebuild me from broken promises, broken marriage, & wasted tears

Rebuild this broken spirit, my broken heart, my broken trust
Rebuild me from the guilt the shame & skeletons I keep in my closet
Rebuild me from my grieving heart & the horrible death of my kids
Rebuild me from the empty feeling of loneliness like:
Nobody's going to love me, nobody wants me, nobody cares
Rebuild me from the brokenness of my thoughts & actions not of You
Rebuild me from the brokenness that I constantly commit:
Rebuild me from anger, excessive alcoholic beverages, backbiting, backstabbing, back-sliding
Rebuild me from the brokenness of cheating on my spouse, controlling behavior, depression, disobedience
Rebuild me from drugs like: cocaine, heroin, crack, sniffing glue, Tylenol pm, smoking cigarettes, smoking weed

114

Rebuild me from filthy communication, gossiping, lying, malice, manipulative behavior
Rebuild me from the brokenness of low-self esteem, self- pity, self righteousness, & pure selfishness
Rebuild me from rebellion, stubbornness, temptation, & unforgiveness

I need You to rebuild me Lord, rebuild my soul and make me whole
Rebuild me and make me in the image You intended since the beginning of time
I know I'm a work in progress but please continue to rebuild me
Rebuild me, take off the old man & rebuild in me a new man
Rebuild me, wash me and make me whiter than snow
Rebuild me, fix me Jesus, and put me back together again
Rebuild me 'cause I know You didn't reject me – I just need to find my reconnection
Rebuild me 'cause I want to present myself a living sacrifice to you
Rebuild me 'cause I've taken what you've made and thrown its value away
Rebuild me 'cause if I harbor all the brokenness, how can Your Spirit stay

Rebuild and replace my brokenness with the fruit of Your Spirit
Rebuild me with love, joy, peace, longsuffering, patience, kindness, meekness
Rebuild me with humbleness, sharing, caring, gentleness, faith,
Rebuild me with righteousness, truth, empathy, hope, happiness, holiness,
Rebuild me with steadfastness, wisdom, charity, forgiveness
Rebuild and replace my brokenness with Your commandments, with loving my neighbor as myself,
Rebuild me with thinking and doing what's pleasing to You, being fruitful in my works for you
Rebuild me with increasing my thirst & zeal in knowledge for You

*Rebuild in me Your work of faith, labor of love, patience of
hope, joy of the Holy Ghost
Rebuild in me a clean spirit
Rebuild me from this brokenness*

REBUKE

Rebuke satan who sends countless temptations
Rebuke him when he sends the young man or lady your way who appears to be
       the 'one'
Rebuke him when he put spirits in your children: clowning in the store,
       breaking curfew, getting smart, talking back, know everything
Rebuke him when your spouse is acting up
Rebuke him when he's next to you in church
Rebuke him when he offer you that one last drink
Rebuke him when the gossipers whisper in your ear
Rebuke him when he's trying to start an argument
Rebuke him when he's disturbing your peace
Rebuke him when he's trying to trick you to rise up against your parents
Rebuke him when he wants you to use profane words
Rebuke him when he tempts you to pick up a little som'em som'em without
       paying for it
Rebuke him waiter takes too long to come back to your table so you duck out
       without paying
Rebuke him from taking a sniff of that white stuff
Rebuke him when he's luring you into depression
Rebuke him when he's telling you it's ok to miss a Sunday because you go all
       the time, you deserve a break
Rebuke him when he makes wrongs justified
Rebuke your weaknesses & temptations
Rebuke your spirit of revenge & bitterness
Rebuke the violence

SAFE FEELING

If you don't feel safe when you look into my eyes
If you don't feel safe when I flash my smile
If you don't feel safe when I put my hand over your hand & squeeze
If you don't feel safe when you hear my voice
If you don't feel safe when I embrace you
If you don't feel safe from using my shoulder
If you don't feel safe from the security of my heart
If you don't feel safe from the kindness of my soul
If you don't feel safe from the passion in my soul

Then maybe something's wrong with you

SECRET HUG

In this poem lies a secret hug

You are definitely my eye candy

Seeing you makes me weak in the knees

You make me wanna beg, "Baby please!"

My stomach bubbles with butterflies,

The words in my mouth get tongue-tied,

My heart starts beating triple-time.

My unconscious mind makes sweet, hot, and steamy dreams

My lips down below flows a succulent stream.

Sometimes when my day feels of gloom,

I see your smile and you light up my private room.

I like the sound of you voice and the way you say, "Hey."

So you do know sometimes it's the simplest things that can make my day?

I inch my way for a secret hug

Now I count from 10 to 1

10, 9, 8, 7, 6, 5, 4, 3, 2, 1

Now that I'm close, my poem is done.

SEXY SINGLE CELIBATE

SEXY
A smile that melts your heart, a walk that gives men wet dreams
Sweetness that's pure & simple, love that's kind and gleams
You see, sexy begins with the inside; great personality & loving heart
If your judgment is based on the outside, you'll fall short.
But yes, to watch me walk away will have you hypnotized
My intelligence will have you memorized

SINGLE
I need chivalry but only if it's from the heart and 2nd nature
A man who will adore me, love me, naturally pamper & nurture
When I'm down, he will be there to pick me up
Realize what a great catch I am, he'll be forever stuck
No stalking cursing drinking gambling, never say good bye
Thinking about me will cause him to have a natural high
He'll protect me, make me smile, trust me; when im upset, he'll hold me
He'll love me, cherish me, caress me, & his shaft will mold me

CELIBATE
Although men beg me please, I knock 'em to their knees, I don't believe in STD's
Although I fiend & pulsate my insides, it's not my time to slip & slide
God will bless me with my Mr Right until then keagles keep me nice & tight
Good smelling brothas, for real brothas, handsome brothas have me contemplating
I'm blessed with wet dreams that help me to resist temptation.
One man for whom I'm appointed life – he will know when he makes me his wife

SHE BEGGED ME

She looked at me with something in her eyes
I've seen that same look from men a thousand times
She finally got nerve to ask me if she could have me for one night
She'd suck me bone dry like a peach that's nice & ripe
She said "you're so beautiful — can I have you please?"
She would make the transition very plain & with ease
I said I'm not interested but why should I choose you over a man
Soft leg/hard leg, plus, a man offers me so much more than you
can
She said "I desire you, I lust you"
She said "please just let me lick u, suck you
And if you want me to stick u, I will put a strap on"
She said "please allow me to caress your breast
She wanted to make my small cup feel like double d's, she'd lick
them her best
She just wanted to touch 'em, tease 'em, please 'em, and squeeze
'em
She said your ass is so perfect I bet its heart shaped in a thong
She just want to grip it & cup it but not for long
She said she wants to watch, touch it, maybe slap it, kiss it, & lick
it cause she's straight mesmerized
She said please just let me touch your caramel skin is making me
lust

She begged me please just let her taste she wanted to put her tongue in endless places

She was becoming desperate to get close to me; she wanted me to feel erotic things

She said please can she play with my tongue ring

Let her experience my lips especially the ones down below

She said please let me taste you while your juice flow

She said please imma go crazy insane cause my mind won't let you go

She said she wants to hear me moan & feel my body shake — nobody has to know

She begged me

SHE SAID & HE SAID

- SHE SAID....y do u look at me so fiercely? ur eyes they pierce me. u stimulate me generate me to ecstasy extremely wet as the sea & ur passion is without ration. what's a girl to do when she's already sprung by u haven't even had u constant thoughts surrounds me - too profound in me. ur sweet kisses penetrate me. ur touch perplexes me my body flintches reflexively. u disturb my peace but u really want is a piece. u throb for me fiend for me - jus doesn't seem reasonable. it's b/c of u i produce large amounts of juice. by the magnetism of ur embrace u have encased me please don't break me. ur animalism knows the best of me jus wait til u get the rest of me.....

- AND HE SAID Wow!
  What you see in my eyes is the hunger, every hour I mentally devour you, eating my way clear through to your soul! I long for the holy waters of your sacred alter to overflow and sate my palate with the fruit of the vine how devine it will be to have you from behind, penetrating deeply into your core in admiration of your spine, see how it arches so your position is prime and ready, my hips rock steady giving you the best part of me, baby you make it hard for me so I'll give it hard to you, but that does not denote difficulty my aim is to slide easily into your pot of honey and be encased in your need to be pleased by tip split you open fluid soakin through the bed sheets while im strokin into the fire!

SMILE

Smile when I hold your hand.
Your smile simply light up my world
You deserve to smile for your new start.
Smile when I can't let go of our embrace.
Can I say something silly & make you laugh?
Can I speak from my heart & make you blush?
Smile because you can't wait to see me again.
Smile so you can continue to light up my world.
You should smile when you daydream about me.
Smile because I'm the reason for your inner glow.
Smile because you just made my day a little brighter.
Smile because we're sharing each others' atmosphere.
I want you to smile because you know I'm your flower.
You deserve to smile to wipe away some years of pain.
Smile because you've found unexplainable happiness in me.
You should smile because I'm smiling because you're smiling.
You should smile because you have the key – key to my heart.
I want you to smile because I'm your sunshine on a cloudy day.
Now I try to think "how can I get this smile for the rest of my life?"
Smile because I found places within you that you didn't even know
existed.
I want you to smile because you just remembered something cute or
sweet about me.
You can even smile because you knows God's secret – that God sent me
as a gift to you.
You'll smile when you describe me to someone; then they'll smile
because they're in awe and they're extremely happy for you or because
actually they envy what you've found.

SNIFF

He sniffed me
He held me then sniffed my neck, then embraced
me a lil longer while in bed
He sniffed me.
He sniffed my chest my belly – spread my legs
(well pried my thighs) &
He sniffed me
I had on blue striped boy shorts only – every
other stripe see through like pee-a-boo
But he sniffed me
Once he pried my thighs – he sniffed what was
between them
He put his nose on my button (you know- the clit)
between the slit &
He sniffed me
Twisted my legs like a pretzel & kissed my ass
while sniffing my ass
Musta been some type of eroticism for him cuz he
seemed to get high off me
And he sniffed
& he grabbed & he touched & he kissed
He sniffed me like I was some cocaine

SPIRITUAL WOMAN & THREE SNAPS UP

Worldly woman wonder where my secret lies
When I try to tell them they act so surprised
Following the Lord has truly made me wise
I say it's the praise in my voice, the spin in my dance
The love in my heart, and the clap in my hands
Cuz imma woman spiritually (snap snap snap) spiritual woman that's me

I walk into the church just as cool as I pleez
Get some hugs, grab me a fan, I may worship on my knees
But when the word is being preached, that's the moment I want to seize
I say it's for the fellowship with God's ppl showing much luv
The blessings that the Lord showers from above
Cuz imma woman spiritually (snap snap snap) spiritual woman that's me

Men themselves often wonder what they see in me
They try so hard but they can't touch my inner chastity
I try to show them God, but those lustful eyes still can't see
I say it's the Jesus in my soul, the sunshine in my smile
I shonuff got the Holy Ghost swagger in my style
Cuz imma woman spiritually (snap snap snap) spiritual woman that's me

Now you see just why my head's not bowed down
I'm Jesus' little sister, there's no need for me to frown
When you see me as God's child, it ought to make you proud
Studying His word gives me knowledge day by day
When I want to be one with Him I fall on my knees and pray
Cuz imma woman spiritually (snap snap snap) spiritual woman that's me

SPOON ME

Spooning is an art few are gifted to enjoy
When my man comes to bed, it's the beginning of a ploy
        We lay in bed happy – happy as can be
        We lye next to each other he – me – we
He rolls over like a positive to negative on a magnet
Not purposely exciting me getting me wet
        His hands slither up my thigh & rest on my hip
        Slides to the side & & squeeze my ass a lil bit
Keeps his hands moving, creeping up my spine
Touching me he starts to moan & whine
        Soft sweet lips on my face & neck
        Here & there he kisses he pecks
I wrap my arms around him to confirm his desire
We're tangled up in each other like two live wires
        My breast pressed against his chest
Stomach to stomach hips to hips legs tangled like spaghetti
I know he wants to tear me up like a machete'
        I flip him & spin around & put my back against him
        Now our bodies form a "S" figure
With his penis growing between my but cheeks
Like he ain't had none for months or weeks
        Our hips our legs, our feet our skin become one
        Wrapped up rolled up with my man is nice & fun
As we lay in bed so happy – happy as can be
We lay spooning, an art to making love, jus he – me - we

STICKS & STONES

Sticks and stones may break my bones but words will never hurt me
But words will never hurt me
But words will never hurt me
Never hurt me

Never hurt me?

Whoever said "word will never hurt me; must have lied or thought that was a good come back
People say things out of anger or hurt or bitterness even orneriness; clearly they don't know how to act

Lying words can cause slander and ruin a person's reputation
Demeaning words can cause a person low self esteem
Cursing words can scar a person deep in their soul
Ugly words can be passed on from generation to generation
Other words can hurt from childhood to adulthood

SUCK YOU BONE DRY

Can I suck you bone dry
So good I'll make yo daddy cry
When I'm finished u cain't do nothing but sigh
Walk around all day like ur on high

I can sit on you & take a ride
U gon think we playin slip & slide
Don't go chasing waterfalls
My sweet juicing gon submerge ur balls

Take my tongue down ur shaft to ur nuts
I'll lick u from ur nuts to ur butt
Toss ur salad like I bought it from rally's
Work up a sweat like u been at bally's

Don't worry about my gag reflex
They become more & more suppressed
When I get done u gon need ur rest
Promise I suck u my very best

Wrap my lips around ur head
U gon be grabbing that headboard on that bed
Sucking & swallowing while on my knees
You gon be begging 'sweetness please'

TASTE ME

You wanted so bad to spend the night with me, and from you, I
wanted the same
But I deemed it prudent if I asked for your last name
I felt like I needed to be wrapped up in your arms
Somehow my heart trusted you would protect me and do me no harm
I snuggled close to you & buried my head deep into your chest
Yes, my spirit & soul found peace and rest
Words can't explain the extraordinary since of security I felt
What's really going on cause next to you – I melt
But you felt compelled to taste me
I held my breath for a few seconds cause I'm nervous as can be
You yearningly asked a 1st & a 2nd time with the utmost respect
You wanted to make love to me in a different way with no neglect
How would this work with clitoris in hibernation
But you went to town like an exfoliation
My back arched as I moaned & bit my lip
While you made your home between my thighs & held firmly to my
hips
Tossed my salad, tongue inside my vagina
Deep tasting licking loving – broke my new hymen
Why would you share with me & allow me to feel this
Did you know the next few days my clit did miss?
When I walked my pants rubbed against her – she thought you were
back for more
I told myself "Girl calm down just don't let him back thru that door
Slap back to reality cause you're on a mission
But I can't help but to fiend for your sweet kissin
You jus can't handle a climax as beautiful as mine
'Cause it's definitely made with love & passion and your heart &
mind still needs time
But when your heart & mind catch up with your lips & tongue
It'll feel so perfect & right – not temporary, or wrong
Make sure that's exactly were they're supposed to be
The next time you put your lips on me & taste me

THANKS FOR MAKING MY DAY

Today was a great day
To see each other you made a way
I don't mean to compromise you
I just fiend for you
We met at this apartment
Just so I could get a quick fix
My heart is pounding, legs got weak
Dang I can hardly speak
I hug you in the middle of the grass
You just had to rub that ass
I'm one step above you
What to do?
In my bosom you rest your head
For a moment nothing was said
You exhale in relief
I have a big grin – showing all my teeth
We're caught up in an intense embrace
Nothing else exists at this time or place
I rub my fingers through your hair
I love your hair but you don't care
You squeeze me like you don't want to let go, make my head spin
Rub my ass once again
I sweet talk you so you'd know what's on my mind
I want you to know you're one of a kind
What the hell is this?
I get more and more moist from your sweet kiss!
Down my neck – up my neck – in my mouth – on my lips
Rub my ass again – grab my hips
I taste your ears & nibble on your neck
With just a few sucky pecks
Your phone keeps ringing and interrupt

I know our time is almost up
     We don't want to leave but we can't stay
          Thanks for making my day

THE BLOOD OF JESUS

His blood reaches from the highest mountain flows to the lowest valley
The blood gives me strength from day to day

His blood washes me whiter than snow
His blood keeps me
His blood carries my burdens
His blood cleans my sins
There's wonder working power in His blood
His blood heals me
His blood was sacrificed for me
His blood purifies me
His blood covers me
His blood is so pure
His blood is of the sacrificial lamb
His blood can reach way down
His blood protects me
The blood still works
His blood fills me
His blood gives us purpose
His blood cleanses me of my wounds, bruises, & iniquity
His blood allows me to be heir to the kingdom
His blood comes from the linage of David
His blood has Holy Ghost power
His blood was shed on Calvary

His blood accuses through my veins
His blood raised me
His blood saved me
The blood of the good Sheppard
The blood that heals a sin sick souls
His blood wounded for my transgressions
His blood protects me
His blood heals from pain & sorrow
His blood heals from heartbreak & heartache

His blood strengthens
His blood gives us direction
His blood gives me purpose
His blood withstands the whiles of the devil
His blood washes away sins
His blood will never lose its power
His blood has power to restore
His blood has keeping power

The blood will never lose its
power
The blood has all power

His blood has wonder working
power
Nothing but the blood of Jesus

I KNOW IT WAS THE BLOOD
THANK YOU FOR THE BLOOD

THERE IS A TIME

There is a time for everything and a season for every activity under heaven
...A time to be born and a time to die, a time to plant and a time to uproot.
...A time to kill and a time to heal, a time to tear down and a time to build
...A time to weep and a time to laugh, a time to mourn and a time to dance
...A time to scatter stones and a time to gather them, a time to embrace and a time to refrain
...A time to search and a time to give up, a time to keep and a time to throw away
...A time to tear and a time to mend, a time to be silent and a time to speak
...A time to love and a time to hate, a time for war and a time for peace
...there is a time to fast, a time to eat, a time to meditate a time to forgive
...there is a time we must back down & humble ourselves and say "I'm sorry"
...there is a time we must bite our tongue and just simply shut up
...there is a time we must tear down old relationship & bad habits
...there is a time we must build great relationships, have better goals, & better habits
...there is a time we need to sit still and wait on the Lord
...there is a time to spare the rod and a time to punish
...A time to get on your knees and pray and tarry; a time to get on your internal knees
...A time to work and a time to retire, relax, and even play

...A time to be selfless & take care of someone else or put someone else needs before ourselves
...A time to trust in God and lean not to our own understanding
...there is a time we hate the sin but love the person
...there is a time we love thy neighbor

> Thy homeless neighbor
> Thy Muslim neighbor
> Thy black neighbor
> Thy gay neighbor
> Thy white neighbor
> Thy Jewish neighbor
> Thy Christian neighbor
> Thy atheist neighbor
> Thy racist neighbor
> Thy addicted neighbor
> Thy imprisoned neighbor

There is a time & the time is now

THIS MUST BE A BAD DREAM

A man just received custody of his 8 year old daughter.

They were walking down the street hand and hand laughing & smiling.

They were about to go into the store just as the light went out.

The little girl stepped ahead but he father was stopped by the officers because the metal detectors alarmed.

The father yelled to his little girl stay to stay right there don't go anywhere.

Two officers frisk him while he said "it's only my pants buckles! Please I need to get my girl!"

He looked through the crowds of people as no one was allowed to leave during this city wide black out.

Then he could no longer see his little girl, but, spotted a man who smiled at him while he walked after the man's little girl.

That didn't sit well with the father, so he became restless & agitated & began to yell at the officers. "If anything happens to my little girl, I'll kill you!"

After frisking him they allowed him to pass. He ran hysterically to find his little girl in the dark through the crowd.

He spotted a curtain just pass the crowd & as he started walking toward it.

His heart was pounding; his little girl came out with her hair all over her head & her clothes disturbed. She fell to the floor & looked up at her dad with her simple smile.

The man came out stumbling with his pants around his ankle trying to pull them up. He looked at the father in satisfaction, relief, & remorse.

The father ran to his little girl & embraced her & wept.

The man fell down before the father & announced, "I'm sick, I couldn't help myself, I'm sorry, please forgive me!"

The man walked out with his daughter.

He looked at the police officers with rage, anguish, hurt, and murder in his eyes.

TOUCH

<u>Before</u> you read this grab some: candles, soft music, oil, gel, maybe Vaseline, Cleopatra's secrets.

<u>Now</u> as your reading this, it's ok to touch yourself. Take the unused hand, reach down & touch it. Is it wet yet? Touch more.

<u>After</u> you're done, do not touch this book. Go wash your hands. Then go to sleep.

Touch Of An Angel

As you lay next to me
    I can plainly see
        You and I are meant to be
My heart was semi-cold & somewhat jaded
    Then you lay your head close to my heart
    And all that faded
You want to know why my heart's beating
        Triple time
I didn't know a touch could be so kind
    Almost thought you were already mine
My soul wrapped around yours; I bet you didn't
know
You tickled my spirit and brought out my inner glow
I couldn't catch my breath as my mind & soul & spirit
    Raised above us and intertwined
They commute with each other & as they look
Down & caught my eye they told me I'll be just fine
Then you kissed me so soft & gentle
    And I finally exhaled
    Like a prisoner who just made bail
If your touch is like that for
    The rest of our life
    I might as well be your wife

TRIFLING ASS

Spreading your legs for every tom dick & harry

Planting ur seeds in every sue sally & mary

TRIFLING ASS

Sharing ur AIDS, HIV, HPV, syphilis, and gonorrhea

Not using condoms, then thinking a douche will cure diarrhea

TRIFLING ASS

Thinking wiping your penis off between tricks will keep u
clean

Stuck it in up baby momma after gettn sucked off by some
whore ass crack fiend

TRIFLING ASS

Can't buy ur kid a pair of shoes but go buy a cell phone

Lay yo hat at erbody's house but can't remember ur own
home

Taking to heart thinking you're a rolling stone

TRIFLING ASS

Tripped up in prison & dropped the soap

Now otta prison gotta man & a woman thinkn that's dope

TRIFLING ASS

Down low ass nigga taking it from the back & the mouth at
the same time

Then going home to hug & kiss the kids like u were at work
doing overtime

TRIFLING ASS

Talking on the cell phone - cheating in the next room

Just finished screwing your spouse but planning a lay with
someone else real soon

TRIFLING ASS

Momma dressing like ebony model from fashion fair

While lil kids look like a poster child for feed the children, half bare

TRIFLING ASS

You running out the back door while her husband coming in the front door

Almost got shot in the ass but tomorrow you'll be back for more

TRIFLING ASS

Dropping your girl off at work, then, over to your other girls house

Already got a hard on thinking bout what you're next pounce

TRIFLING ASS

You want your woman to invite another woman in your ménage a trios

Double standard when she wants you to invite another man in her ménage a trios

More trifling when you want your girl to watch you & two other men in your ménage a trios

TRIFLING ASS

You had the nerve to invite your lover to your wedding

More trifling she bought you & your wife a wedding gift

TRIFLING ASS

Beating your woman like she's a human punching bag

Tryna compensate for being insecure, low self esteem, & 5 minute man

TRIFLING ASS

This type of karma has a way of fulfilling your own destiny & coming back around

Pre-destination won't build up - it'll just tear you down

TRIFLING ASS

TURBULANCE – the moment after peace of mind just before working my nerves

You know I'm not a morning person – don't call me before 10am
You've just caused me turbulence

If we're having a conversation and my smile turns to "what the…"
You probably just caused me turbulence

When I tell you I'm not ready for a relationship – don't ask me
where I been, why I didn't answer my phone, that's turbulence I can
get rid of real fast

If we go on a date & I say good night, don't ask if you can come in
for a cup of water
I run from that turbulence

When I give you a hug & I break loose cause I can feel my body heat
draw toward you in radiation
I run from that turbulence

Don't complain about your job everyday for the past 10 years – look
for something that's gone make you happy – you're causing me
turbulence

When I'm in my zone getting my crazy leg on, don't ask me to
couple skate
That turbulence causes me to lose my rhythm

Just because I smile at you does not mean I want to have sex
You're causing me turbulence

If we're on the highway I'm to the left of you and someone's in front
of you & you can't pass, I will hit my breaks to accommodate you
I don't need unnecessary turbulence

Don't be 30 years old living with your parents and no job, but talking
bout you're going to take care of me, & that you're a good man
You're causing me turbulence

If I get a headache cause your mouth is moving but you're saying nothing
You're causing me turbulence

Don't tell me you're a 45 minute cleaners but I have to put my clothes in before 10 am, and I can't get them back til after 4 pm.
You're causing me turbulence

Don't do research after I've practiced good eating habits for years then you wanna tell me turkey bacon & pork bacon are pretty much the same but turkey bacon has lots more sodium
You're causing me turbulence

When I build a circumference around me by extending my arm that's my space – if I can smell your breath, you're in my space – you're causing me turbulence

If we're in the middle of smooching then you have to use the bathroom & I didn't hear the faucet run for you to wash your hands – we cannot pick up where we left off – you caused me turbulence

If we're in church & you know you're one of those shouting brothas or sistas - please sit in the front pew so you cannot step on my feet – you're causing me turbulence

If I go to your house & I have to squat like I'm at a gas station restroom you're causing me turbulence

If you need to argue, fuss, complain, look ugly I in the face all the time you're causing me turbulence

If you can't bring me peace, joy, laughter, love, hugs, smiles. You're causing me turbulence

TYPE OF LOVE TOO

I want that type of love – I want that type of love that when I'm having a screwed up day he feels it in his soul right away and he calls me on the phone & ask how can he make it ok – that type of love
I want that type of love where we're mentally, physically, soulfully, & spiritually connected
I want that type of love in the morning b4 we get outta bed he doesn't mind a little head, oh yeah – that type of love
I want that type of love b4 I go to work he embraces me like he'll never see me again, no matter how bad of a day he had at work, when he walks thru the door & sees my face he lights up
I want that type of love that for no apparent reason other than "it's Monday" he sends me a dozen of stargazers or African lilies or multi-colored tulips

I want that type of love because he was in love with God 1st, he knows this woman's worth he accepted God's gift to himself, and befriended me 1st
I want that type of love where he understands God didn't take bone from man's head so woman cud be above him – in charge of him, nor did He take it from the many bones in the feet so she cud be beneath him – walked all over by him, but He took it from his rib – the side of him- to be closest to him, to be protected by him, to be nearest to his heart to be loved by him
I want that type of love that when I'm feeling down, he finds out what's gotten me off pace & if he's the reason, he makes sure he puts that smile back on my face
I want that type of love when he looks into my eyes, he speaks to my soul
I want that type of love when he still opens the doors for me, falls asleep on the phone with me, talking bout "you hang up, no you hang up, on 3 we hang up"

I want that type of love when its cold outside we've got the month of May

I want that type of love when he knows that just because we have sunny days don't mean it won't be some rainy days but together we can weather the storm
I want that type of love that when it can't always be 50/50 he pulls 30 I pick up 70, til he gets back on his feet and vice versa – that reciprocity type of love
I want that type of love where he wants me time after time, he still wants me like every time is our 1st time – that type of love
I want that type of love there's no fussin & the only cussin is in a heat of passion

I want that type of love while making love heaven opens and descends of doves – that type of love
I want that type of love afterwards, we can't move, can't breathe, can't speak all we can say is – owee – that type of love
I want that type of love when I'm at work I smile off into space 'cause I just felt his cum from this morning run outta me
How many of you have really been in love? I mean really been in love?
When u talk u get tongue – tied & in ur stomach there's butterflies. Now how many of you been in love like that?
I want that type of love after I've eaten his home cooked meal, he massage my feet, digs his thumbs in deep, makes me weak I begin to moan then cut of the phones cause it's about to be on

I want that type of love when I use him as a punching bag, even tho it's not his fault he's not mad, but because of my hurt he's a little sad, til I come back to him & say – "aa ba ba, my bad". That apologetic type of love
That type of love that makes me humble & say "baby I was trippin u no it's not too many times I be slippin" that forgiveness type of love
I want that love where I know I'm no beauty queen but he see the beauty deep within me & to him I'm the most beautiful woman in the world.
I want that type of love where he doesn't believe in conquest but his delight is in the discovery of me
I want that type of love where the safest place for me is in his heart
The only questions is "where are you"

UR BEAUTIFUL

Ur skin is like a chocolate raging river flowing as a
gentle stream
Ur smile lights up my heart, when u enter, it beams
    3 suns describe ur smile with the greatest
    illumination
    Ur magnetic force, forces my thoughts to expel
    mental ejaculations
        Ur voice is cool – calm as a gentle summers'
        breeze
        It's mellow, soft, subtle, puts my whole body
        & spirit at ease

Ur eyes pierce deep penetrations that reach the soul of
me
I feel ur touch without u touching me because u have a
spiritual hold on me
    Chocolate brown sugar with each kiss of ur lips
    renders me breathless
    Thinking of u, missing u, fiending for u – leaves
    me restless
        U musta been thrown those bones, or put a
        root on me or used a magical balm
            Cause wrapped up in ur arms
            renders me light-headed & my
            palpitations calm

Ur laugh reminds me of honey molasses with sweet
epiphany's
When I see u I wonder what lies beneath
    I visualize ur goals & my goals intertwined as one
    dream
    I only wish I was worthy to be ur queen
        Cause I know in ur heart is the safest place
        And I want to be there – not this hopeless
        case

WE DANCED

We shared a slow dance, a momentary love romance
But it was our time & in my mind
It was jus u & me, I closed my eyes & I — felt — u
My face layed against ur face, as I pulled u close into my space
Ur chest pressed firmly against — my breast
 Our hips joined 2gether like twins of Siamese (thought I felt ur seeds)
We met at bilateral thighs, while I'm lost in natural highs
I warned u as soon as u let me go I wud go home
So u pulled me in & held me tite — you did not leave me alone
And we danced
There were lots of people all around
Jus grooving to the DJ's great sounds
But that music — I cud not hear
Close to u wrapped up in ur arms I had no fear
Cause the music in my head came from the rhythm of ur heart beat
When ur blood pushed from ur atria to ur ventricle I felt that beat
Every other heart beat caused a shift in my feet
And we danced
It seemed like 4ever since I've been that close to any man
I remember so vividly as I felt 1 slow stroke of my hair from ur hand
As our hip swayed simultaneously side to side
What I was feeling down below — dang that was just fine
Jus like silk or satin sheets the sweat from ur body was smooth
I didn't even care 'cause I was feeling ur groove
Somebody tapped u on the shoulder
And said, "man slow songs been ova!"
U turned back to me, pulled me back to u
And we danced

WET DAYDREAMS

I've made love to you a 1000 times
        Even though, it's all in my mind
                You make me feel a strong desire
                      To set your soul on fire

My daydreams are plain to see
        That you bring these emotions out of me
                As I visualize watching us in the mirror
                      Inner-twined as we shiver & quiver

I play with you, caress you, kiss you,
        Tell u how much I've missed you
                I hold you touch tease you
                      Lick you please you

I rub you ride you slip in slide
        Feel you deep inside me boo
                I suck you & taste you
                      Make you cum 2

It's so vivid in my mind
        As I can see you cumming inch by inch inside
                Letting your juices flow free
                Deep within me
                      We lay naked as could be

I've made love to you a 1000 times
        Even though it's all in my mind
                A 1000 times & then sum
                And this is only one

WHAT JUST HAPPENED?

I awakened tied down spread eagle. At first I could not see. My vision blurred in and out as I tried to focus. "I hear noises in the background; some rustling like newspaper or plastic or both." I struggle to get loose. It was very hard. I dislocated my thumb & that allowed me to wiggle my hand out. I hurried to loosen my other arm & both legs. I'm in pain. I see bruises all over my body, blood on the bed & smell of blood in the air. My insides feel like a burning sensation; in my rectum and in my vagina. I don't know where I am, what happened, how long I been here.

"shhhhh! I hear footsteps! They're coming back to finish me off! I hear his voice! 'She should be waking up again.'" I held on to the rope like I was still tied up. He leaned into me. Before I knew it, I had grabbed him with my free arm & bit into his neck. He reflexively put pressure on his bleeding carotid. While he was stunned, I freed myself & ran around the house like a maze. I ran into a lighted room & searched frantically for a weapon – anything. "Yes! A shotgun." I loaded it & cocked it. He evidentially heard it in the almost hollow place because he tried to escape me. Funny, how the script was flipped. I heard keys & the house door opens.

I ran after him while he darted to the car. I saw a can of gasoline sitting on the porch with a utility lighter. I dropped the shotgun, picked up the can & lighter. Just before shutting the car door I doused him with gasoline. He kicked me hard in the stomach & it caused more pain & caused me to stumble. But I managed to pour gasoline over & around the car, as he was fumbling with the car keys. I lit the car on fire & backed away. Within seconds, he & the car were ablaze. I fell to my knees and watched him. He struggled to put himself out. I ran to the porch for the shot gun & ran back. I kept a close aim on him just in case he managed to put it out. I just watched & listened to him as he screamed in agony. Finally, he stopped.

WHAT MANNER OF MAN IS THIS

What manner of man is this?
Who could co-exist as part of the Trinity..

What manner of man is this?
Who would travel 42 generation to save you& me..

What manner of man is this?
Who could transform from the Spirit to the Flesh..

What manner of man is this?
Who would volunteer to stay here 33yrs until His horrific death..

What manner of man is this?
Who can heal the sick & raise the dead..

What manner of Man is this?
That even the winds obeyed what He said..

What manner of man is this?
When in the midst of a storm, can say, PEACE BE STILL..

What manner of man is this?
That the oceans & seas obeyed His will..

What manner of man is this?
Who hears & answers ours prayers..

What manner of man is this?
That knows our worries & feels our tarries..

What manner of man is this?
Who can heal from a simple touch of His garment..

What manner of man is this?
Who heals from all power – not from some magical performance..

What manner of man is this?
Who can walk on the waters..

What manner of man is this?
That lead by example according to our heavenly Father..

What manner of man is this?
Who could raise Lazarus from the dead..

What manner of man is this?
That life & death is obedient to what He says..

What manner of man is this?
To forgive us without a 2nd thought..

What manner man is this?
To give us chance after chance
When upon ourselves anguish we brought..

What manner of man is this?
To love us unconditionally
Although we constantly do wrong..

What manner of man is this?
To look Satan in the face & say BEAST BE GONE..

What manner of man is this?
Who would lay – His- life – down..

What manner of man is this?
Who would sacrifice freely
When He wasn't obligated or bound..

What manner of man is this?
Who would suffer a beating & torture
Just for being His perfect self..

What manner of man is this?
Who would love pitiful us even long after His death..

What manner of man is this?
Could rob death even from His own grave

What manner of man is this?
To arise in the name of the Father, Holy Spirit, & His own name..

What manner of man is this?
Who gives us clothes, shelter, & food to eat..

What manner of man is this?
To leave us His word for our spiritual meat..

What manner of man is this?
To go to Calvary to save a wretch like you & me..

WHAT'S WRONG WIT CHA

My guy call me & asked what I was doing, I said "studying"
He said, "well I might as well stay at work then…"
        So when he gets home, I was studying in the dining room and he
        Comes over to me and starts squeezn & rubbin & touchin & kissin
He says "…you didn't tell me you were studying butt naked."
I said, "I guess I'm through studyin, but, What's wrong wit cha?"

Next day he calls & ask "what cha doing?"
I say I'm in bed bout to shut it down
        So he says he'll be home in a couple of hours
        So later I hear him coming in the door so I lay across the bed
Purposely facing the window. He comes in the room & is like
"Oh my God" & drops his bag cause my lovely lady humps are in pink see
        Thru boyshorts, so 1st he had an eye full, then he gets two hands full
        Then a mouth full, I say, "baby, what's wrong wit cha?"

The following day his boys call him on the phone & all I hear is one way
I hear him say, "…naw man….I'm good…got something else to do…."
        Then he turns over & squeeze me rub me touch me, jus all ova me
        I flip him on his back & he enters me. I pull a surprise from under my pillow
And I cuff one hand to the bed & he whisper, "no baby no" so I raise and
Come down on it and I say, "yes baby yes" now he's weak & he can't resist
        My neighbors call the police. Now they're knockin on the door talking bout
        "We know ur in there; come out with ur hand up!"
I say, "baby you need to learn how to be quiet "what's wrong wit cha?"

I'm sleepin in the bed, I woke up to find myself mummified
  Not only was I being spooned but I was in a death grip
        One arm around my neck the other around my waist
        Leg wrapped around my legs. So I shout, "let me go I cain't breath..I gotta
        use it"
He says, "how long u gon b? when u comin back? Hurry up I miss u already.
I say, "dang I'm jus goin to the bathroom, what's wrong wit cha?"

Another night I get home at 3am & he triiiiied to get mad at me
Talkn bout 'where u been, what took u so long, u cheatin on me, yadda yadda…'
        I flicked his earlobe w/ my tongue-ring and my tongue-tip & started kissin his
        Neck, put my hands down below, pulled down his pants,
Got on my knees and …(you know the rest)
So I go to the bathroom cause before I go to bed I like to groom
        When I came back into the bedroom, he was curled up in a ball like he was
        in his mother's womb. I said, "boi get up and go to bed! What's wrong wit
        cha?"

The next day I said, "We need to talk. What's really going on? Are you crazy about
me? Are you in love with me? Are you sprung? Are you in lust with me: baby, are you
Henpecked? But what I really wanna know is WHAT'S WRONG WIT CHA?"

When A Tree Falls

If a tree falls in the forest does it make a sound?

What difference does it make?
What about the squirrels from which the tree supplied their nuts?
What about the rabbits who shelter their babies in safety?
What about the birds that used to sit on the branch of that tree & sing?

Did that tree fall on somebody who tried to yell for help while their bones were being crushed?
Did that tree fall on several animals, killing God's creatures?
What about the oxygen exchange that supplies our daily life?

What about the beauty that trees possess that can't be duplicated?
What about the shade it provided in the heat of the summer?
And what about the place it supplies for our kid to play hide & seek?

WHO KNEW

You didn't imagine that you could fall so fast
You didn't cut me short because of things in your past
    You could not have perceived that you'd ever
    fall so deep
    Now you're messing around trying to play for
    keeps
You have yet to feel how you'll fall so hard
Just so happens that destiny said this love is in the
cards
    You thought you may have been in love once
    before
    But your soul is craving for so much more
You fiend to have me by your side
Your facial expression shows things you just can't hide
    You may even get afraid sometimes
    Because you can't seem to keep me off your
    mind
You want me to be in your life forever & always
Even in our golden old days
    God sure did send you a gift that's one in a
    million billion
    But He gave me you —and you're one in two
    zillion

WHY DO WE SING

Someone asked a question- why do we sing
When we lift our hands to Jesus, what do we really mean?
Someone may be wondering when we sing our song
At times we may be crying and nothing's even wrong.

I sing because I'm happy, I sing because I'm free
His eyes is on the sparrow so I no He watches me
Glory glory hallelujah he's the reason y I sing
Glory glory hallelujah such joy these songs bring

I sing because, I just wanna praise Him, forever & ever & ever
For wakin me up this morning and keeping me through the day
I sing because I jus can't praise him enough
I sing because He guides me and watches me along the way

There's a blessing in the storm - there's a blessing in the storm
There's a blessing in the storm – help me sing it

If God always saved us from the storm
We would never know that he can save us in the storm
No trouble ever last 24/7-365 this is the part in our lives
When we only see one set of footprints in the sand, we must realize

The footprints are too big to be ours, He carries you
Just like the 3Hebrew boys in the book of Daniel, He carries you
Shadrach, Meshach, & Abednego, he carries you
And will stand up for you when you stand up for Him

We enter into His Holy steeple
Not for the benefit of a show or the people
If he has to reach way down – I mean way down
Jesus can pick you up

No matter the time or region
He keeps those who claim "I don't have a closet religion
I can't hide the God I serve I have to let the world know
Wherever I go, I have to praise and serve the Lord"
AND THIS IS WHY WE SING

Woo Man ~ Woman

In the beginning God created the heavens and the earth
& on the sixth day God created man & called him Adam
But God saw that he was lonely and caused him to fall into a deep sleep
Then He conferred with the other two (the Holy Spirit & Jesus)
And He said, "Let Us create beauty, let us create perfection"
And he took a rib from Adam & formed a new vessel.

When they woke up, Adam saw her and said, "Woo man!"
And as Eve walked around in her nature around nature,
She observed God's beautiful garden.
And as she walked Adam observed her natural sway & said, "Woo man!"

Nonetheless, Eve became mother of many nations & the template for all women:
Strong woman, timid woman, intelligent woman, sensual woman,
Fine woman, big boned woman, petite woman, curvatious woman,
Tall woman, short woman, singing women, dancing women,
 Fabulous women, educated women, super women, wonder women,

Classy woman, eccentric woman, brave woman, powerful woman
Chaste women , nurturing women, loving woman, sanctified woman
Humble woman, praying woman, preaching woman, virtuous woman
And we are pearl, olive, midnight, black, chestnut, brown, honey, bronze,
Coco dipped, big lipped, big hipped, God fearing & beautiful all at the same time...

With all Gods' grace & infinite wisdom, God has anointed uniquely designed women.
To this day men are still mesmerized & hypnotized by our natural sway
And when we walk pass he says...Woo Man ~ Woman.

163

CONCLUSION

I hope at least one poem in this book appealed to you

Dontjudgeme.com / lol ☺

Any questions on why I wrote a particular piece or what inspired me or you would like for me to perform a piece at your event: birthday, church, reunion, etc., please contact me at sk8ntj@gmail.com or on face book "Tea Jay"

SPECIAL ACKNOWLEDGEMENTS

THANKS TO ALL WHO AGREED TO HAVE THEIR NAME IN MY BOOK AND/OR RECOGNITION FOR INSPIRING SOME OF MY PIECES: Kelly C, Antoian Johnson, Borope Rashad, Corey W, Lisa Camp, KK, Nessa, Joe Rice, Gregory Khalil Flenoid, Derrick Sutton, David (Damo) Morris, Greg Johnson, Anad, Larry Blissit, Todd W, Nique, Mari, Trey, Bubba, Ms C Godfrey, Mikii Hooper, Craig Butts, momma, Mikki, CC, lil D, Ms Nterpretation, Chris Ware, Rodney Davis, Shauntel Jones, Rundell (16 Bars) Irvin, Enoch Raavi, David Moran, David J, Marlon M, Fifi (Kisobo) Yuma

DISCLAIMER

This book is anywhere from 0% to 100% fiction or non-fiction however you look at it. Written on a thought, a picture, or some phrase heard in a conversation or in passing. I apologize to anyone who may be offended.

REFERENCES

Beatitudes Matthew 5:3-10
http://www.biblestudytools.com/kjv/matthew/5.html

Box of Chocolates movie "Forest Gump", 1994

Can I Lay In Your Arms Donald Lawrence "Get Your Life Back",
2002

Dem Bones Ezekiel 37:4 &5
http://www.biblestudytools.com/kjv/ezekiel/passage.aspx?q=ezekiel
+37:1-14

Did You Get Fully Dressed Today Ephesians 6: 11-20
http://www.biblestudytools.com/kjv/ephesians/passage.aspx?q=ephe
sians+6:11-20

I'm in Love With a Man Romans 8: 38 & 39
http://www.biblestudytools.com/kjv/romans/passage.aspx?q=roma
ns+8:38-39

I'm Spoiled Joss Stone "Mind Body & Soul", 2004

My Prayer is to Heal the Land Rain New Direction 2004, 2
Chronicles 7:14 http://www.biblestudytools.com/kjv/2-chronicles/7-
14.html

Order My Steps Gospel's Top 20 Various Artist, 2001

Our Father Matthew 6: 9-13
http://www.biblestudytools.com/kjv/matthew/passage.aspx?q=matth
ew+6:9-13

Press On Mark 5: 27-29
http://www.biblestudytools.com/kjv/mark/passage.aspx?q=mark+5:2
7-29

Rebuild Me "Just James" J. Moss, 2009

Spiritual Woman 3 SnapsUp, Mya Angelo's Phenomenal Woman &
an anonymous writer

There Is A Time Ecclesiastes 3: 1-8
http://www.biblestudytools.com/kjv/ecclesiastes/passage.aspx?q=ecclesiastes+3:1-8

What Manner of Man is This Matthew 8: 27, Mark 4: 41, Luke 8: 25
http://www.biblestudytools.com/kjv/matthew/8-27.html;
http://www.biblestudytools.com/kjv/mark/4-41.html;
http://www.biblestudytools.com/kjv/luke/8-25.html

Made in the USA
Columbia, SC
25 November 2017